CARDBOARD CITIZENS PRESENTS

MINCEMEAT

Written by Adrian Jackson and Farhana Sheikh
Directed by Adrian Jackson

15 June – 12 July 2009
Performed at Cordy House
87-95 Curtain Road
Shoreditch
EC2A 3AA
www.cardboardcitizens.org.uk

APPROXIMATE TIMINGS

Act I   100 mins
Interval   20 mins
Act II   30 mins

After show bar: The Hoxton Pony
(Opposite Cordy House)

CARDBOARD CITIZENS PRESENTS

MINCEMEAT

Written by **Adrian Jackson** and **Farhana Sheikh**
Directed by **Adrian Jackson**

A site-specific production at Cordy House.

Mincemeat was first performed in June 2001. This new production is the
first in a three-year cycle of plays about forgotten histories, all based on
real events in which an ordinary person affects a bigger sweep of history.

Girl in Film **Rebecca Brown**
Animal 9/Johny Bevan/Maureen **Linda Dobell/Terry O'Leary**
Animal 3/Head Official/Maria/Lorena **Ester Escolano**
Animal 1/ Schicklgruber/Pam/Maud/Molly **Jo Galbraith**
Old Montague/Charlie **Robert Gillespie**
Animal 4/Translator/Agnes/Cholmondley/Firestarter **Jakob B Goode**
Animal 8/Montague/Dai **Nicholas Khan**
Ivor Leverton/**Ivor Leverton**
Animal 7/Major Martin **Ifan Meredith**
Animal 5/Lt Jewell/Fred Shrieve/Private Secretary/Gerry **Patrick Onione**
Animal 2/Speech Trainer/Obituary/Workman/Glyndwr **David Rogers**
Animal 6/Churchill/Foreman/Alf **Ben Smithies**

Mincemeat is performed by a professional cast including ex-homeless actors.

Designer **Mamoru Iriguchi**
Music and Soundtrack **David Baird**
Movement **Linda Dobell**
Bombsite Movement and Refugee Videos **Emma Bernard**
Lighting **Zerlina Hughes**
Producer **Jeremy Goldstein for London Artists Projects**
Production Manager **Sheelagh Barnard**
Assistant Director **Pierre Becker**
Assistant Producer **Stuart Grey**
Voice Coach **Tim Charrington**
Casting Associate **Lucy Jenkins**
Costume Supervisor **Carolyn Horn**
Company Stage Manager **Victoria Hambley**
Deputy Stage Manager **Eavan Murphy**
Assistant Stage Manager **Talia Scholar**
Sound Engineer **Tom Parkinson**
Technical ASM **Morgan Fox**

Marketing Consultant **Mobius 020 7836 3864**
Press Agent **Sharon Kean 020 7354 3574 sharon@keanlanyon.com**
Internet film trailer **Daniel Saul**
Box Office and Ticketing Services **Soho Theatre 020 7478 0100**

Producing Interns **Abena Adofo** and **Theresa Pine** of Creative
Producing course, Birkbeck, University of London, Stratford

BOMBSITE AND SHELTER: Miguel Barros, Patrizia Carlota, Kieran Saikat
Das Gupta, Kenneth Eyo, Jenel Gregg, Sidney Griffiths, Jamil Haque,
Christopher Heimann, Chris Holland, Shara Ismail, Ian Kalman, Amie
Kamara, Kareem Khan, Sayed Wali Khan, Fred Meller, Abraham Neguze,
Lidya Neguze, Stuart Nicklin, Kerry Norridge, Terry Osman, Diene Petterle,
Beatriz Pinto Francois Preira, Philip Robinson, Fifi Russell, Katie Sage, Lydie
Salima, Anthony Sandy, Ksanet Sengal, Siratoullah Shirali, Freddie Still,
Emma Symes, Tigisti Tesfazion, Eriseld Toska, Abdullah Varfar, Melanie
Vickers, Hekmat Sakhi Zadeh.

Thanks to our volunteers: Simon Anderson, Joseph A Canny, Liz Clark,
Howard Davies, David Hamilton, Jane Gauntlett, Anthony Larson, Matt
Lavin, Oskars Lazurka, Shane Nolan Tanner, Philip Robinson, Fifi Russell,
Freddie Still, Agnes Tomilson, David Walker, Darren Wooley.

Special thanks to Nick Allan, Melody Allen, Rebecca Brown, Natalie Cain,
Richard Edwards, Ceryl Evans, Cressida Finch, Hadrian Gerrard, Garfield
Hackett and Liam Hayhow at Artcore International Ltd, Christopher
Heimann, David Isaacs, Sylvia Larry, Ivor Leverton, Roy Luxford, Diane
Petterle, John McPherson, Cllr Jonathan McShane, Fred Meller, Shahro
Motvaliam, Roger Morgan, Cllr Guy Nicholson, Phil Reed, Noreen & John
Steele, Simon Thomson, Natasha Wallace, Chris Westwood, Victoria
Williams, The Hoxton Pony, Blitz Sound, Blitz Vision, Digital Village, Pains
Plough, Royal Marines Museum, Tricycle Theatre, Wieden + Kennedy.

DIRECTOR'S/WRITERS' NOTES

No-body and Some-body – Mincemeat

In *The Great Dictator*, Chaplin's Jewish Barber saves a German officer's life in the First World War, only then to suffer an amnesia which takes him back to his old life in the ghetto with no consciousness either of his heroism or the terrible attack on his community. Fortunately he then meets the officer he saved, who becomes his protector. Later in the film, having escaped from captivity, he is mistaken for the dictator Adenoid Hynkel – his stolen uniform gives him credibility – and is suddenly placed in the position of powerful speechmaker. Chaplin seizes this opportunity to talk to the world – it is clear from the delivery that this is no longer just the character speaking, but Chaplin himself. All protective layers of irony are peeled away to allow Chaplin to make an appeal for humanity which feels as relevant now as ever.

At Cardboard Citizens, we have tried always to find the larger historical arc within which the little man or woman at the bottom of the heap fits. This is partly an effort to counter the still prevalent notion that homelessness is a pathological condition, perhaps related to drugs or alcohol, and that, whilst society should of course help these poor souls, they are unlikely to be in any way pivotal in our history or existence. Somewhere in the genesis of this project, which actually started with the exposure of the story of Major Martin, I became aware of the centrality of the homeless experience to Hitler's story – and then coincidences and overlaps flowed from there. Charlie Chaplin came into the mix comparatively late in the day, but he too found his place in the telling of this story. The Tramp has always been iconic for me, but I was unaware of Chaplin's bravery in making *The Great Dictator*, which he financed himself and made against all the odds, or the way his own trajectory tracked that of Hitler.

Hitler and Chaplin were born in the same year, within seven days of each other. Both men experienced extreme poverty, Chaplin as a child in the workhouse, Hitler as a young man in Vienna, where he became a tramp, slept rough, and stayed for two years in a hostel supported mainly by Jewish charities. Chaplin's Tramp makes his first experience on film in 1914, when Hitler was about to have his first experiences of war in the trenches. Hitler was of course eventually to be invalided out of that war after a gas attack, an event strangely mirrored in *The Great Dictator*, not by the autocratic Hynkel, but in the long First World War sections of the film featuring the amnesiac Barber and his subsequent convalescence.

Both men went on to exercise an incredible influence on the world, with huge popular followings; interestingly Hitler failed to move people in silent film propaganda, requiring the addition of his familiar machine-gun guttural demagoguery, so superbly parodied by Chaplin, before his popularity really took off. Chaplin was speaking for the first time on film in *The Great Dictator*, after years of successful silence. and it is here that their identities converge: Chaplin plays both Dictator and Barber, thus the mistaken identity. The swastika becomes the Double Cross. Though Chaplin's films were banned in Germany, we now know that Hitler watched *The Great Dictator* twice in the dying days of the Third Reich, down in the bunker.

In the latest of the many coincidences we have encountered in making *Mincemeat*, at the time of writing this programme note, I found out that *The Great Dictator* may well have had its genesis at the prompting of a good friend of Chaplin's who sent him a copy of a German anti-Semitic tract, *The Jews Are Looking at You* in the late thirties. The sender was one Ivor Montagu, communist-leaning brother of Ewen Montagu, the distinguished member of the London-based Double Cross committee responsible for deception operations in the Second World War and the man who knew Major Martin best. The riddling of *Mincemeat* goes on.

ADRIAN JACKSON
27 May 2009

Even the dead will not be safe…

When I was writing my contribution to the play, I had some of the ideas of Walter Benjamin in mind. In the Spring of 1940, Benjamin, an exile from Germany, trapped on the border between France and Spain, took his own life. (Unlike Glyndwr Michael, he found the Spanish frontier impassable.) In his last work, Benjamin had written that it was the past, not only the present, that was endangered by fascism: 'even the dead will not be safe from the enemy if he wins'.

His argument extended beyond fascism. Rulers are always 'the heirs of those who conquered before them'. They have enormous empathy for their predecessors, and very little for the defeated: official history was a 'triumphal procession in which the present rulers step over those who are lying prostrate', and every document of civilisation had as its underside a record of barbarism.

Mincemeat is not unconnected to Benjamin's vision. Its sympathy is for the 'prostrate'; its concern for the unsafe dead.

FARHANA SHEIKH
27 May 2009

Who on earth are you?

You are who people say you are/You are who you say you are.
You are what you have/You are what you eat.

DAVID BAIRD – MUSIC AND SOUNDTRACK
Composer/Writer/Director – People say I take on too much, sleep too little.
Eat well… Exercise? Ha! They say they like my music, I'm not certain why. People
bought 10 million of my books…I ask 10 million more whys? I am Welsh, no I am
Canadian… I am Polish, no…none of these really and yes all passionately. Certainly
I am a loving father. There are people I love and have loved and lost. I try to avoid
hate. I have been homeless, I have been married, been displaced and artistically, I
seem to find myself best when I am all at sea!

SHEELAGH BARNARD – PRODUCTION MANAGER
Rather a personal question: what do people say you are? It's gratifying to be valued
but mostly I just hope that people will get me. I am an optimist. I have a strong
sense of myself. Work is important. I like to be part of something that moves or
provokes people. I think opera can be sublime. I collect small, resonant objects and
images but live very simply in an attic. I wander. I take photographs. I cook. I drive
too fast. I like to be alone a lot but love my friends. There is never enough time.

PIERRE BECKER – ASSISTANT DIRECTOR
People see me as French. Some people think I am too French, some people think I
am not French enough. People think I spend my life cooking French food, drinking
French wine and singing 'Non, rien de rien'. But the fact is I can't cook and I love
hamburgers so am I really French?
I possess nothing. I share everything. I share my life with my partner, and good
times and difficult times with my friends. Whoever I am, 'je ne regrette rien'.

EMMA BERNARD – BOMBSITE MOVEMENT AND REFUGEE VIDEO
I say: I'm a theatre maker, a community campaigner, a mother, daughter and wife.
People say: I'm tenacious, bolshy, sometimes harsh, passionate, friendly, anxious
and strangely calm.
I have: a handbag full of keys, pencils, biscuits, insulin, notebooks, lists, lipsticks,
oyster cards (3) and a multitude of unsorted receipts.
I'm a bowl of rice, not a loaf of bread.

LINDA DOBELL – MOVEMENT/ANIMAL 9/JOHNY BEVAN/MAUREEN
I hope I am evolving, Too slowly for some. Too slowly for me.
I have luck with people, mostly.
Food is fuel, if I'm lucky enough to keep it down or up.
Slow, mostly lucky.

ESTER ESCOLANO – ANIMAL 3/HEAD OFFICIAL /MARIA/LORENA
My friends say that I make up my own rules. They say that I am talkative but I know
I can be very shy in front of strangers. I have a body that tells people more than I
want them to know. In front of food I lose my humanity and I become feral. I am
only sometimes unstable but always crazy. The reason for this is simple: 'I was born
in June under the twins'.

MORGAN FOX – TECHNICAL ASM
People say I am a very strange person. This is due to the fact that I do on occasion
express my confusion by cocking my head and barking, some may say this is
because I grew up with two dogs in my household or because it was the easiest
way to talk to my baby brother.

JO GALBRAITH – ANIMAL 1/PAM/MAUD/MOLLY

I am Joanna Faith Catriona Galbraith, a name too long to fit on most application forms. I am a mother, a daughter, a sister and a partner.
I am a failed vegetarian who can't resist the odd bit of cow once a week.
I am an activist, an actor, a performer and a protester. I meditate and cycle and recycle. I have a home, good health, friends, community and a rat.
I am a rabid ex-smoker.

ROBERT GILLESPIE – OLD MONTAGU/CHARLIE

Since other people's view of me is greatly coloured by what they want from life for themselves, I anchor myself as a member of a species of anthropoid ape – in my case *Homo sapiens* – evolved so as to effect my particular birth for which I did not ask. Finding myself astonished at what people find it worthwhile to do – like shut themselves in offices and try to acquire huge tracks of land – I sidelined myself to become an observer in the arts…an actor and occasionally a writer…a means of exploring whether there is an attractive way for our species to one fine day, conduct himself – or whether to simply watch the looming collapse (I've been amazingly fortunate, because it'll happen after I'm gone).

JEREMY GOLDSTEIN – PRODUCER

I am what I eat – rich, spicy, sweet, sour, bitter, hot, cold, à la carte, junk, fast, delicate, tender, rare, exotic, local, take-away, international – take your pick – I am complex and committed to them all. I am also a product of the house I love and live in – London. Each day I think I might know where the rooms are, but suddenly I stumble on a door I didn't know was there. I'm surprised but not afraid to walk in and turn the light on, where almost always I become someone new.

JAKOB B GOODE – ANIMAL 4/TRANSLATOR/AGNES/CHOLMONDLEY/FIRESTARTER

My parents said
I am 'Martin John Goode',
Martian Baptist of naked equestrian extraction perhaps,
but my son calls me 'Dad',
and my partner: 'Jake', amongst other things.
For Equity's sake Jake Could B. Bad
And on such days
I circumvent
Self-imposed banishment of domestic flesh
By eating out
Reluctant omnivorousness (sic) excluding
Boiled, fried, poached and scrambled eggs;
GMOs:
And people.
On Goode days I am an auto Gnome of the suicidal Earth species,
Misnamed *Homo sapiens*;
Imagination determinedly deriving possibility from ownership of a body of
Instantaneously disappearing, and
Re-appearing
quantum matter.
Which it does, or I wouldn't be here
Or so I'm told.
I think.

STUART GREY – ASSISTANT PRODUCER
I am Stuart David Grey.
My grandfather was a rear gunner in WW2.
I am the youngest of three siblings. My mother says I was a gift from God.
I eat music and theatre and drink three pints of water a day.
I am hungry.
I own one pair of trousers which have a large hole in them.
I need a new pair of trousers.

VICTORIA HAMBLEY – COMPANY STAGE MANAGER
I have a balcony and an occasional pet.
I have one TV but hundreds of books.
I have a fridge full of healthy food but don't have the willpower to turn down chocolate or crisps if they appear within reach.
I have an oven I don't know how to use but a boyfriend who uses it on my behalf.
I have family in Canada and the US but have friends all over the world.
I have lots of shoes but hate shoe shopping…I don't know how that happened…
I have no interest in mediocrity.

CAROLYN HORN – COSTUME SUPERVISOR
Mother, friend, yoga practitioner, yoga teacher, sibling, aunt, maker of special clothes for special people, gardener, violin player, lover of textiles, maker of bread, costumier, comforter, great aunt, advisor, host of garden parties, maker of feasts, lover of wild flowers, admirer of the human body, admirer of all bodies, questioner, collector of hand made textiles and artifacts, (especially from the Silk Road), lover of music from Bach to Glass, and of course the London Gypsy Orchestra cos I play with them.

ZERLINA HUGHES – LIGHTING
You are what people say you are,
Trained at Goldsmith's and the The Bartlett School of Architecture. Worked as a lighting designer in theatre opera and dance both nationally and internationally productions *La Vie Parisien* (Malmö Opera), *Dead Man Walking* (Copenhagen Opera House), *The Abduction from the Seraglio* (Opera North).
You are what you say you are.
Someone who is interested in telling stories visually.
You are what you have.
I have two amazing children and we love living up the road in Stoke Newington.
You are what you eat.
In which case I am almost everything.

MAMORU IRIGUCHI – DESIGNER
I see myself as a transparent human-shaped container that stores a record of decisions I make every day till the end of my life.

ADRIAN JACKSON – DIRECTOR/CO-WRITER
I am the son of a German Jew who came to England in the 1930s, who afterwards translated books about that history, but died when I was 15. I have always wanted to understand more about the war. People would say I am quite argumentative, impatient, irritable verging on the great dictatorial, but I think I am very patient. I have a house, a car, a family, all that. I have an absence of memories from childhood. Food is important, I eat and cook everything, it's how I relax. I started Cardboard Citizens.

NICHOLAS KHAN – ANIMAL 8/MONTAGU/DAI

I am a Londoner, I love its parks and the calming influence of the River Thames. My father was born in Bangladesh – a delta country with five rivers coursing through it. My mother is English, a Londoner too. I have a brother. I have a partner and a son who is our future.

The sea has always been a significant something to me, and water offers a solution in defining me. Like water – a motion, willful, mercurial, connecting in eddies, collecting, an echo of an other.

My mother recounts the story of her grandfather, the captain of a tug who 'apparently' fell overboard in the Thames. 'Was that true?' I asked my mother. 'Things weren't said in those days love' she replied.

In life I motion through sometimes free, and maybe connected by the notion we are echoes of others.

IFAN MEREDITH – ANIMAL 7/MAJOR MARTIN

My name is Ifan Meredith, but my friends sometimes call me 'The Goldfish' because of my woeful short-term memory. My own personality has always seemed to me somewhat beyond my reach which is part of why I enjoy pretending to be other people I think. I nurture a slightly guilty penchant for Heinz spaghetti hoops on toast with melted cheese on top, which is a hangover from my childhood. I see myself very much as a Welshman although the initial impressions of strangers are often very much at odds with this.

EAVAN MURPHY – DEPUTY STAGE MANAGER

I see myself as someone who is very passionate about her job and about life. But I am also a hopeless romantic, and that was the reason I left the comfort of home to live in London. I love travelling and conversation. I know my big downfall can be how opinionated I am at times, but I would never judge someone for believing in something that I don't. People say that I am temperamental at times (this is true!) I possess a lot of happy memories. I eat a lot of chocolate in ANY shape or form, it's an easy way to get on my good side.

TERRY O'LEARY – ANIMAL 9/JOHNY BEVAN/MAUREEN

I am the eldest daughter and a twin. I am a Londoner, south Londoner. I have performed and taught throughout London. I am a joker. I have worked in Israel, Greece, Holland, Norway. I make theatre. I am a forum theatre performer. I have seen *The Lower Depths*.

PATRICK ONIONE – ANIMAL 5/LT JEWELL/FRED SHRIEVE/PRIVATE SECRETARY/GERRY

My full name is Patrick Daniel Cochise Onione. Although my grandfather was Italian and Onione sounds Italian his name was Manze. My grandmother's maiden name was Onions. My father changed it to O'nione. I don't know why, maybe he wanted to sound Irish, I don't know. I subsequently took off the apostrophe making it sound more Italian. None of this messing about with our name has made any difference because we have always been called Onions. The Cochise is a whole different story.

Other people say I am a Bermondsey wide boy or a Millwall supporting thug. I have my nose down in wet grass, with a smile on my face, and my head in the clouds. I eat life.

TOM PARKINSON – SOUND ENGINEER

Kind-hearted, pop-experimentalist, hedonistic-anarcho-Marxist, pro-fox-hunting vegetarian musician WLTM sexy atheist who gives blood.

I have no idea what anyone says about anything. I am a musician, my ears are made out of wet asbestos. Safe to love because I already love music and chips and such. My name is Ken Buddha. Last year and a bit of this, I lobbied to close a loophole in the law that allows for eviction of tenants by lenders without notice. It worked. The institution of government and the brains of its workforce, however, are inedible.

DAVID ROGERS – ANIMAL 2/SPEECH TRAINER/OBITUARY/WORKMAN/ GLYNDWR

I am both Dave and David. I am a Yorkshireman and thus sometimes misunderstood by southern ears that hear directness as aggression. I am an organiser of five-a-side football. I'm not sure whether it would serve me better or worse to speak RP all the time. I like sardines. I am a socialist. My sister's brilliant.

FARHANA SHEIKH – CO-WRITER

I am: a novelist (*The Red Box)*;
a playwright (*Arabian Nights*, *The Flood* etc);
a Lahori, who does not live in Lahore;
a Londoner, who does not live in London;
a foreigner, who writes about the West;
a feminist, who writes about women: sweatshops, Scheherazade;
and about men: Gilgamesh, Gulliver, Glyndwr Michael.
I have: a British passport; a house; some money.
I eat: enough, more than many.

BEN SMITHIES – ANIMAL 6/CHURCHILL/FOREMAN/ALF

Contrary to people's perception of me, I am a contradictory person: as soon as I believe something I can see that the opposite might be equally true. I may be a wave or a particle, we cannot be sure.

Other people say that I have a sense of humour. Yet after some long and hard experience I feel I must speak with the utmost restraint and caution about myself as it is a subject about which I can get bogged down. I feel able to declare that I possess many things but thankfully no cats. I love all kinds of food excepting (in its uncooked form) the radish: food holds a sacrosanct importance in my life since I have lived in France, Italy and India.

I am in truth a lazy man, often late: but I try to love all people.

TALIA SCHOLAR – ASSISTANT STAGE MANAGER

I am my mother's daughter: stubborn and determined. I direct the course of my life with the influences of my friends and family around me. I'm a hard and passionate worker and enjoy what I do, whether its theatre productions, live music or events. I'm not really sure what people say about me and perhaps it is better not knowing. My friends tell me I'm good to them because I care, and I do, about them, my family and my work.

I eat traditional home-made Jewish Mediterranean/Moroccan food made by the inspirational, hard-working women of my family.

I have a goal and a dream that I want so much and everything that I do and every job that I undertake will hopefully lead me to my ambition.

CARDBOARD CITIZENS SUMMER BLITZ

Cardboard Citizens presents a series of events to coincide with *Mincemeat*:

KEEP IT UNDER YOUR HAT: A Night In The Shelter
Saturday 16 May | From 6pm – 8am
The Churchill Museum & Cabinet War Rooms SW1A 2AQ

Families sign up for an overnight night stay in the Cabinet War Rooms. Performers from Cardboard Citizens workshops will bring the historic rooms to life during the event.

Director **Emma Bernard**
Designer **Sophie Jump**
Sound **Jeremy Cox and Reynaldo Young**
Stage Manager **Rachel Reeve**

KEEP CALM AND CARRY ON
Saturday 30 May | 6.30pm & 8pm
Sunday 31 May | 6.30pm & 8pm
The Churchill Museum & Cabinet War Rooms SW1A 2AQ

A promenade performance in Churchill's underground bunker, devised by young refugees and asylum seekers in response to *Mincemeat* and the history of homelessness and displacement during wartime.

Director **Emma Bernard**
Dance Artist **Joe Moran**
Costume Designer **Sophie Jump**
Stage Manager **Rachel Reeve**

MORE BUMS ON SEATS
Saturday 20 June | Doors 7.30pm, 8pm start
Hackney Empire E8 1EJ

A cheeky evening of stand-up comedy with Stewart Lee, Richard Herring, Simon Amstell, Brendon Burns and Josie Long, with all proceeds to Cardboard Citizens.

'CORONERS' INQUESTS': Two Public Inquiries into the Death of a Man Who Never Was
For these two fact-based inquiries, audiences join actors, pathologists, forensic scientists and historians in investigating the truth about the identity of Major Martin and the use of his body in this remarkable wartime deception.

WHO WASN'T THAT MAN?
Tuesday 23 June | 5pm followed by *Mincemeat* at 7.30pm
Cordy House EC2A 3AA

FUNERAL RIGHTS?
Monday 29 June| 6.30pm for 7pm
The Churchill Museum & Cabinet War Rooms SW1A 2AQ

For further information or to book please visit
www.cardboardcitizens.org.uk

Thanks to the following funders and supporters of *Mincemeat* and associated events

CHURCHILL MUSEUM
and CABINET WAR ROOMS

Wieden
Kennedy⁺

CARDBOARD CITIZENS

Cardboard Citizens is the UK's leading professional theatre company working with homeless people. Founded in 1991 by Artistic Director Adrian Jackson, recent productions include *Woyzeck* at Southwark Playhouse, and with the RSC – *Timon of Athens*, *Pericles* and *Visible,* by Sarah Woods.

As a nationally and internationally important theatre company, rooted strongly in its local community, Cardboard Citizens makes a positive contribution to many people's lives.

Wherever possible, the company employs ex-homeless people. In addition, 10% of our tickets are given away each year to people who have experience of homelessness or social exclusion.

If you would like to become a friend of the company by donating as little as £3 per month, please visit www.cardboardcitizens.org.uk

Friends receive up to date information about the work of Cardboard Citizens, plus priority invitations to future public performances and events.

Cardboard Citizens

26 Hanbury Street

London

E1 6QR

Tel: 020 7247 7747

Email: mail@cardboardcitizens.org.uk

Web: www.cardboardcitizens.org.uk

Registered Charity Number: 1042457

I am delighted and proud to be working with Cardboard Citizens as their Ambassador. Over the last 16 years they have managed to pull off that very rare trick of producing artistically excellent work that challenges audiences at the same time as making a real difference to people's lives.
Kate Winslet, Cardboard Citizens Ambassador

CARDBOARD CITIZENS STAFF

To email our staff send a message to firstname@cardboardcitizens.org.uk

Director of War & Homelessness **Emma Bernard**
Director of Development and Marketing **Lisa Caughey**
General Manager **Michael Gaunt**
Administrator/PA/Assistant Producer **Stuart Grey**
Artistic Director and Chief Executive Officer **Adrian Jackson**
Finance Manager **Jonathan Kaunda**
Associate Artist **Terry O'Leary**
Development Manager (Grants) **Valentine Leys**
Membership Officer **Lucy Martin**
Programme Director **Tim Nicholls**
Data Administrator **Yago De La Torre**
Project Manager (Hostel Workshops) **Cathy Weatherald**
Project Manager **Tracey Weller**

BOARD MEMBERS

Mojisola Adebayo
Treasurer **Mary Rebecca Blackwell**
Sian Edwardes-Evans
Andy W Ganf
Mary Ann Hushlak
Chairperson **Dan Mace**
Barbra Mazur
John Moffatt
Philip Parr
Gaynor Quilter
Sue Timothy

SUPPORTING CARDBOARD CITIZENS

PUBLIC BODIES

Cardboard Citizens would like to thank the following funding bodies for their vital support:

London Development Agency

Arts Council England

London Borough of Tower Hamlets

London Councils

British Council

TRUSTS & FOUNDATIONS

Cardboard Citizens would like to thank the following trusts and foundations for their recent support:

The A B Charitable Trust

The Ashden Trust

The Baring Foundation

The C M F Charitable Trust

The City Bridge Trust

The City Parochial Foundation

Clacton Quakers

The David King Charitable Trust

The Dischma Charitable Trust

The D'Oyly Carte Charitable Trust

The Gibbs Charitable Trust

The Harley Charitable Trust

The Harold Hyam Wingate Foundation

The Heritage Lottery Fund

The Hilden Charitable Fund

The Hiller Charitable Trust

The Hyde Park Place Estate Charity

The J&D Hambro Charitable Trust

The Joan Strutt Charitable Trust

The Kemble Charitable Trust

Lawrence Atwell's Charity

The Leaver Family Charitable Trust

The Margaret Guido Charitable Trust

The McPin Foundation

The Monument Trust

The New Court Charitable Trust

The Odin Charitable Trust

The Peter Courtauld Charitable Trust

The Radley Charitable Trust

The Reuben Brothers Foundation

Richard Cloudesley's Charity

The Russell and Mary Foreman Charitable Trust

The Sir Jules Thorn Charitable Trust

The Syder Foundation

The Trusthouse Charitable Foundation

Trust Greenbelt

The Tudor Trust

The Wakefield and Tetley Trust

The Wessex Youth Trust

The Westminster Amalgamated Charity

The Worshipful Company of Butchers

COMPANIES

Thank you to our corporate supporters for making their financial resources and expertise available to Cardboard Citizens.

Ashridge Consulting

Bradford and Bingley

Makinson Cowell Limited

Penguin Group

Wieden + Kennedy

UNDERCOVER
UNCOVERED

LIFE IN CHURCHILL'S BUNKE[R]

27 August 2009 – 30 September 201[0]

70 YEARS
1939-1945

IMPERIAL WAR
MUSEUM

CHURCHILL MUSEUM
and CABINET WAR ROOM[S]

[F]or details and to book visit www.[i]wm.org.uk/cabin[et]

he Official After Show Bar

...and it's just over the road!

resent your MINCEMEAT ticket stubb to ain swift entry into the venue

o claim your 15% discount on drink nd 10% discount on food show your MINCEMEAT ticket stubb at the bar or to our server!

e have an extensive bar menu with the finest cocktails!

e serve delicious East End grub with a twist till 10pm mon-fri!

Opening hours:
12pm-1am mon-thurs
12pm-2am fri
5pm-2am sat

THE
HOXTON
PONY

020 7613 2844
info@thehoxtonpony.com
www.thehoxtonpony.com

MINCEMEAT

First published in 2009 by Oberon Books Ltd
521 Caledonian Road, London N7 9RH
Tel: 020 7607 3637 / Fax: 020 7607 3629
e-mail: info@oberonbooks.com
www.oberonbooks.com

A catalogue record for this book is available from the British
Library.

ISBN: 978-1-84002-935-2

Printed in Great Britain by CPI Antony Rowe, Chippenham.

Characters

AGNES

ALF

CHARLIE

CHOLMONDLEY

CHURCHILL

DAI

FIRESTARTER

FOREMAN

FRED SHRIEVE

GERRY

GIRL IN FILM

GLYNDWR

JOHNY BEVAN

LT JEWELL

HEAD OFFICIAL

IVOR LEVERTON

LORENA

MAJOR MARTIN

MAUREEN

MARIA

MAUD

MOLLY

MONTAGUE

OLD MONTAGUE

OBITUARY

PAM

PRIVATE SECRETARY

SPEECH TRAINER

SCHICKLGRUBER

TRANSLATOR

WORKMAN

ANIMAL 1

ANIMAL 2

ANIMAL 3

ANIMAL 4

ANIMAL 5

ANIMAL 6

ANIMAL 7

ANIMAL 8

ANIMAL 9

Act One

SCENE 1

The audience standing around in a downstairs space. An old-fashioned phone on a girder rings, till it jumps off the hook. And we hear:

RECORDED VOICE: You know that feeling when you wake up and you don't know where you are, you don't know what you've done, you're not sure if you might have committed some awful crime –

and sometimes it stays with you all morning –

what have I done…with my life?

Pause.

(*From elsewhere.*) Mincemeat –

A huge commotion, with loud music, as double doors to street open with much noise and screeching of tyres. Three people in plastic animal masks bundle in, followed by hippy van reversing in.

1/3: I'll get the doors/Squirrel, check the other rooms/Help me with the doors/In here/Careful/Shut the fucking gates/ Turn off the fucking engine.

They are in. 2, 7, 8, 4, 5, 6, 9 bundle out of van. Much celebrating: 'we did it!' 'yeehaah,' etc. Then they are manhandling a coffin from the van into the centre of space. One gets a crate to place it on. All wear cheap plastic animal masks. Many of following conversations are overlapping.

2/8/1: Ok, lets get him out./Put him there. /Easy does it.

The other major thing going on here is the setting up of the video etc. which is designed to video the kidnap victim.

9: On the chair.

7: What is this place? (*7, 8, 9 go rooting round.*)

1: Some kind of factory I reckon, sweat shops probably.

7: Sweat the working classes, why not?

9: I used to go clubbing round here.

6: Shakespeare's first theatre was here.

9: Remember the old Whirlygig.

5: Yeah, great days.

6: It was in the papers….

7: You don't want to believe everything you read in the papers mate.

4: Rags of the capitalist lackeys.

3: It's not old enough, Shakespeare is like a hundred years old.

5: The whirlygig of time brings in his revenges.

6: I don't mean this was his theatre, stupid – I mean it was on this site.

7: He's not moving.

2: He's not dead is he?

1: Don't be stupid.

4: Get him out.

From the coffin, they carry out the body of an old man, wearing a hood and big padded headphones.

8: We'll have to do an autopsy.

6: Is there a pathologist in the house?

2: Call Betty Purchase.

4: Let's get that bloke who did the poor homeless fucker at G20.

8: Police pathologist been totally discredited.

5: Died of a heart attack.

4: Yeah right.

1: They're on like their third post-mortem.

5: (*Having a piss in a corner.*) To pee or not to pee, that is the question.

1: Must you?

5: Bursting mate – hanging around in the van waiting for them to come out the funeral.

6: They reckon he did *Henry the Fourth* here.

9: A hearse, a hearse, my kingdom for a hearse.

6: That's *Richard the Third.*

9: Oooh – listen to fucking Melvyn Bragg here.

6: *Henry IV* is the one with Falstaff, and Hotspur, and the Welsh rebellion.

1: Make sure he's tied up good and tight – he's a wily old bugger.

2: Intelligence, remember.

4: Everyone ready?

2: OK.

4: Shhhhh. (*They start filming.*)

8: I officially declare this space from forthwith a Temporary Autonomous Zone or TAZ.

5: A what?

6: A temporary autonomous zone.

8: This Temporary Autonomous Zone is open –

7: Long live pirate utopias –

5: Fuck the system.

3: Que se vayan todos! Out with them all!

6: Fuck the system!

8: And did those feet, in ancient time, walk upon England's mountains green?

5: More free festivals!

1: Can everyone SHUT THE FUCK UP !

8: Heil Hitler!

1: Oh, right –

2: Can we just start thinking about what this is going to look and sound like when we put it on the net?

8: I was being ironic.

2: Come on.

4: And again?

8: This temporary autonomous zone is open.

1: And our first guest in this Temporary Autonomous Zone is –

They de-hood and de-headphone the kidnap victim, who is a sixty-something year-old man, EWEN MONTAGU.

M: Where am I?

7: The TAZ.

M: The what? Why have you brought me here?

2: To tell you a story.

M: You kidnapped me to tell me a story.

1: To bring back some memories.

4: Your memory, our memory, the national memory.

7: The memory of a man whose memory was lost.

6: And everyone wonders who he is.

7: Including him.

M: A man who lost his memory?

9: You got it.

M: What on earth is that to do with me?

3: What's anything to do with anyone else?

8: We are all isolated ions, discrete particles, banging and vibrating against each other…in this eternal void.

5: Bollocks.

1: It's something from your past, come to haunt you.

M: What?

2: That's for you to guess and us to hide.

4: Deception – that's the name of the game. Should be familiar enough to you, Commander Montagu.

M: You know my name.

2: Of course we know your name. We know a lot about you. MI5 aren't the only ones with files, you know.

7: Every step you take, every move you make, I'll be watching you.

M: You do realise the seriousness of what you've done… I am a judge, a high-ranking judge.

9: Oh, yes, you're the judge who said that 'boy criminals should be spanked' –

1: – 'minus trousers' –

9: 'with a hair brush by women police officers.'

2: 'Photographs should be taken and exhibited in every local café and coffee bar.'

6: 'I am certain that this would kill half the juvenile crime in the country at once.'

M: You don't mean to tell me that you people have kidnapped me because I made a slightly ill-advised quip in a summing up twenty years ago?

8: A slightly ill-advised quip!

7: Yeah right – we represent the Provisional Wing of the WPC's Benevolent Fund.

M: You're terrorists.

5: One man's terrorist is another man's liberation fighter.

3: Another woman's liberation fighter.

M: Oh for God's sake – (*Laugh*.) are you women's libbers?

6: He's a brave old bird, you gotta hand it to him.

M: Do you intend to ransom me – I'm not a rich man.

2: Oh come come Commander, you made a few bob from your book.

8: Thirty-thousand pounds in 1956, according to documents lodged in the Public Records Office –

5: A lorra lorra money.

M: Who on earth are you?

1: Rogue historians.

2: Freelance undertakers.

7: Toxic avengers.

8: We're anarchists, your highness.

M: Anarchists?

2: We're an anarchist militia.

6: You know – Like in the Spanish Civil War.

4: Kropotkin.

3: Bring down the Capitalist conspiracy.

6: Shelley, the POUM.

M: The POUM were communists, you bloody idiot, not bloody anarchists.

5: Oooooh.

4: Trotskyists actually.

M: What do you know about Spain? I knew people who died in Spain, good people –

3: Well I am from there actually. My Grandfather was fighting during the war.

5: I am an Anarch-yst, I am the Anti-Christ.

M: Absurd – absolutely absurd, the lot of you.

7: 'Absurd – absolutely absurd'.

M: You're the sort of people who go round smashing things, daubing statues, blocking the roads with your bicycles, breaking the law…

1: Oh, breaking the law, eh? Well you should know about that.

M: Because I am a judge?

2: Before you became a judge, you worked in Intelligence.

   Silence.

7: It's all gone quiet over there…it's all gone quiet over there.

9: He's lost his memory.

5: Bad case of amnesia.

M: I will not talk about my time in Intelligence.

4: Well we will then – you were Lieutenant Commander Montagu, were you not? Working in Deception, Section 17M, London Controlling Section.

M: It is public knowledge that during the war, I worked in Deception – and I left directly after it, so if you think I am some kind of active spy –

2: And when you worked in Deception, might you have done a few teency-weency law-breaking things?

Pause.

M: It was wartime. If we hadn't had the freedom to act as we saw necessary, you young people wouldn't be here today –

7: (*Old codger voice.*) I died in the war for you.

M: It's completely different from the sort of wanton chaos you lot get up to. *Silent leges inter arma.*

3: Eh?

1: 'Laws lie quiet when in arms.'

M: I prefer 'Among weapons, laws fall silent'.

5: Anything goes when you're in charge?

3: So what's the difference with what we do?

M: The difference, young lady, is that we were fighting the bloody Nazis, that's the difference.

3: Well we're fighting a war too, old man.

M: Against?

4: Against you, against smug bastards like you, against all those who have, on behalf of all those who have not, on behalf of all the child labourers slaving for the multinationals, and all the innocents blitzed by your bombers, and all the homeless masses huddled in doorways around the world.

3: Smash globalisation, smash the G8!

6: (*Singing.*) Arise ye starvelings from your slumbers etc.

M: You people are contemptible.

1: Look Commander M, we are not going to hurt you and we are not going to ransom you, we just want to document a few answers to a few questions, and then we'll let you toddle back to your happy family in Kensington.

M: What is my crime?

1: No major crime that we know.

9: You ain't no big time war criminal.

3: Or prime minister.

1: Just a certain economy with the truth.

2: A refusal to acknowledge heroism albeit unknowing.

8: And a little lie which you kept telling longer than you needed to, which might cause one to wonder whether a larger lie was hiding behind it.

M: What?

1: The man who never was.

4: Tell us the truth about what happened to him? In a warehouse like this, in St Pancras, in January 1943.

Silence.

M: This isn't going to work.

4: What?

M: This isn't going to work... It's completely illogical.

9: Hey!

M: If you are going to construct a fiction, it has to be believable to the people you want to deceive.

3: (*Private.*) Is this Montagu or Robert?

M: Montagu died in 1986, way before we had anarchists running riot on their bikes and planting tents all over the Square Mile.

The fiction of theatre has been dropped, people start removing masks.

1: Oh you are so wrapped up in bloody logic and naturalism.
– Dave?

2: Actually, I agree with Robert.

1: Oh for God's sake.

2: I felt stupid doing it.

4: Me too.

8: And me.

1: Jesus – gang up, why don't you?

8: Apart from the dates being wrong, its absolutely ridiculous
to imagine that a group of anarchists would kidnap
Montagu just because he wrote a book about something he
did in the war and didn't share the profits with the relations
of its subject. It's completely out of proportion.

VIDEO: (*Being played back.*) Montagu died in 1986 –

2: You can't kidnap someone who is dead.

9: We're not really kidnapping him.

7: We are sort of kidnapping him, he was a real person, when
we embody him on the stage, we are kidnapping his
reputation, projecting our views onto him – what right do
we have to do that ?

5: You don't see a parallel?

7: I see a parallel, I'm just not sure it's right.

1: Oh fine, well you try then, someone else try, someone
else try.

3: Anyway, you're missing the point, that isn't why the
anarchists kidnap him, it's a gesture, it's a way of making a
statement about the value of a life.

6: I thought it was quite dramatic, quite a good way to begin.

9: Oh dear oh dear oh dear.

M: Well you see that's the trouble with anarchy, you can't agree on anything.

1: Oh please don't start that again.

Space.

4: (*To audience.*) That was what is known as 'a false start'. It might have been that sort of play, but it's not.

2: Thank God.

9: Had you going though, didn't we…?

7: Next false start.

10: Who on earth are you?

9: Walk this way, we'll start again next door.

SCENE 2

NOTE: this is a transitional scene, a preface to the real story, in which the actors as themselves tell many related stories, some of themselves, mostly of parallel/overlapping stories to those of the characters in the play, mostly connected with memory loss and homelessness. Hitler and Churchill are introduced in unexpected ways.

ALL: (*They self-define.*) I am a this, I am a that…

VOICEOVER: Mincemeat.

9: This a story of many stories, a riddle with the layers of an onion. Most of it is true. Some of it we made up. But we only made stuff up where we were not allowed to know the truth. Because there isn't anything written in the official history.

6: Acting is making things up. Acting is pretending to be someone you are not.

5: Is it?

6: It's therapeutic, being someone else.

5: Is it?

3: You are who people say you are.

9: You are who you say you are.

4: You are what you eat.

8: You are what you have.

1: (*Imitating Old Montagu.*) Who on earth are you?

7: On earth, as in heaven, amen.

5: During the evening we will be acting, playing with our identity. And the main story is about a man trying to work out his identity. You will have to use your imagination, we can't afford the costumes, we can't afford the accents.

The company are lined up in short order, and an instructor, 2, drills them with posh voice exercises. For instance, recitation in 1950s posh of: 'an oyster is annoyed by noise. What noise annoys an oyster? Dirty purple curtains Potato tomato potato tomato'. This is live, and spontaneously led by a harsh task-master. The people the instructor picks on are interrupted and have to repeat till they get it right, it might involve the audience.

9: Years ago Cardboard Citizens did a play called *The Lower Depths.* This play might just as well be called *The Upper Echelons* – a sort of companion piece. But it's not. It's called:

Chorus.

ALL: Mincemeat.

2: Some dossiers on some dossers,

8: or 'some files on some flakes'.

7: I knew this squatter, thought he was the reincarnation of a medieval Welsh freedom fighter, Owain Glyndwr – who rebelled against Henry the Fourth and was proclaimed by his followers the Prince of Wales, – 'because', as my friend never tired of saying, 'they never found his body see, Owain Glyndwr never really died'…

3: If he believed that's who he was, where's the harm ?

5: When I was living in the hostel, this bloke is always banging on and on about one conspiracy theory after another. He says:

4: (*As conspiracy theorist.*) before World War Two the Nazis worked with the Rockefeller Foundation on their first programme of calculated killing, on the principle of eugenics, kill off the weak and degenerate, preserve the fittest.

5: And this programme apparently turned into the murder of the Jews, except that the Rockefeller foundation couldn't afford to be seen to be involved,

4: so they did it all with this Eugenics Society, and after the war it went on with the same people, but it changed its name and then after a bit it became respectable again, and now its called the Human Genome Project,

5: and we're all going to be on file, we're all going to be ID'd and who knows what'll happen, if it turns out you're weak or 'degenerate'…

9: Am I paranoid or is everyone out to get me? Eh? Eh? Eh?

10: Conspiracy theory – covers everything – and it's probably true…

8: Best to take no notice of people like that – it only encourages them.

6: In 1909, somewhere in Middle Europe, a lice-ridden man arrives at a large recently established doss-house for the homeless, 'Asyl für Obdachlose'.

10: Literally 'Asylum for those without shelter'.

6: Asyl für Obdachlose –– where he rants on every subject under the sun –

1: (*As Schicklgruber.*) I used to smoke, used to spend all my money on fags. I spent months without ever having a hot meal, I lived on milk and dry bread. But I spent thirty kreuzers a day on my fags, smoked between twenty and forty a day…till one day I reflected that with five kreuzers I could put some butter on my bread. I threw my fags into the Danube and I've never smoked since. Will power.

9: One day this bloke let slip that his father's name was originally Schicklgruber, changed his name before this bloke was born – well, once they knew about the Schicklgruber thing, they gave him some serious stick.

Various actors taunt Shickelgruber.

2: (*Shouted.*) Oi, Schicklgruber, get over here –

9: But this bloke can really talk back, talk the hind legs off a donkey this bloke, talk about anything, hours at a time, didn't care if anyone listened or not –

1: I had a dog, Foxl, my best friend he was. I first met him chasing a rat, and he fought against me and tried to bite me, but I didn't let go. I led him back with me…and gradually I got him used to me, by giving him biscuits and chocolate…and I started training him…and he never went an inch from my side…till some bastard from the railway stole him.

9: But this bloke wouldn't answer to the name of Schicklgruber –

3: What was the name he used then?

9: He answered to the name of Hitler.

1: Drunkards are easier to deal with than sober people – give me the undisciplined swine who is drunk eight hours of every twenty four in preference to the puritan any day of the week. The man who spends extravagantly, the old bastard who drinks and smokes without moderation, such a person is obviously less to be feared than the drawing room bolshevist who leads the life of an ascetic.

4/8/7: Heil… (*Beat.*) …Schicklgruber!

2: As luck would have it, later in life, he got duffed up by a podgy alcoholic pensioner who drank like a fish, day and night.

3: And what was his name?

2: Our Winston –

6: (*Performs extracts of Winston's 'We'll fight them on the beaches' speech and others about halfway through following speech and the two fight volume-wise. Possibly also 'Hitler has only got one ball'* [1] *sung.*)

1: The idea of struggle is as old as life itself, for life is only preserved because other living things perish through struggle… In this struggle the stronger, the more able, win, while the less able, the weak, lose. Struggle is the father of all things… It is not by the principles of humanity that man lives or is able to preserve himself above the animal world, but solely by means of the most brutal struggle.

7: Eh?

4: You remember old Schicklgruber?

2: A sandwich short of a picnic.

9: Loopy loo.

8: Off his rocker.

3: Louca.

5: Meshuggenah.

---

1   Hitler has only got one ball, Goering, has two but very small, Himmler, is very sim'lar, and poor old Goebbels, has no balls, at all. (To tune of *Colonel Bogey*).

2: In 34 years' time he will commit suicide, because he knows he's lost it –

7: And Churchill?

6: 'I dreamed that life was over. I saw – it was very vivid – my dead body under a white sheet on a table in an empty room. I recognised my bare feet projecting from under the sheet. It was very life-like…perhaps this is the end.'

2: That's what he said in 1945. Lived another 20 years, as it happens.

4: You know that feeling when you wake up and you don't know where you are, you don't know what you've done, you're not sure if you might have committed some awful crime.

10: I knew I was in London, I knew that much.

4: And sometimes it stays with you all morning.

10: For some time I went around the place, on the tube, on buses, thinking that I would see something which would trigger my memory, some hint of the familiar, at which all the other missing details would fall into place. I passed some months in this way before I was recommended to a day centre.

8: The true and unconnected story of a minor politician who lost his memory in 1999:

10: By now I probably no longer even resembled the person I had been, so the likelihood of being recognised by anyone was even less than before. Then, I was approached on the street by a fellow politician, a man on the other team, to whom I was probably quite rude.

8: (*As the politician.*) You cunt.

10: That's right – (*Happily.*) I called him a cunt and he called me a cunt and everything was back to normal.

2: Amnesia is usually triggered by some kind of trauma. Individuals, nations even, may experience events they wish to forget, and this results in amnesia.

5: I drink to forget.

2: In one version of amnesia, called a 'fugue state', an individual may 'flee' from his usual life circumstances and take on a completely new identity. He becomes someone else altogether, and has no memory of his 'real' self.

7: Some people are running from who they were or might have been, some people are running towards who they might become.

1: And most of us are somewhere in between.

2: Do you really want to know who you are? Why? Ignorance is bliss, yes?

5: No, ignorance is piss.

10: Perhaps it's safe to say…we ignore people at our peril…you never know who is going to turn out as what.

4: A history lesson.

ALL: Mincemeat.

7: (*The Actor playing MAJOR MARTIN later.*) You know that feeling when you wake up and you don't know where you are, you don't know what you've done.

5: (*Guiding audience.*) Come this way please.

7: you're not sure if you might have committed some awful crime –

5: (*Beckoning audience.*) Come this way.

7: and sometimes it stays with you all morning –
    what have I done with my life?

The audience process upstairs. On their way up they may be asked to empty the contents of their pockets into plastic bags which they then carry with them.

As the audience is travelling, they may well hear again…

VOICE: you know that feeling when you wake up and you don't know where you are, you don't know what you've done, you're not sure if you might have committed some awful crime –

and sometimes it stays with you all morning –

what have I done…with my life?

The distant sound of 'Let him go, let him go' – taken from the burial at sea scene later in the play.

SCENE 3A

The audience arrive at a space which is a cross between a dole office waiting area and the gates of Heaven. As they enter, they are given numbers, which correspond to years. There are rows of seats facing three desks with angels at them. None of the angels looks like an angel (no wings or anything). Two angels are going round with tea. Others are doing other angelic things, including greeting people. 'We'll Meet Again' plays on the piano. In amongst the audience, on seats, clutching his number, is MAJOR MARTIN.

GREETERS: Hello, good morning, bonjour, buon giorno, guten morgen, gin dobre, hello, etc.

ANGEL 1: (*Same in unfamilar languages.*)

When audience is arriving, someone is at main desk being processed. This involves questions etc., followed by the emptying of pockets and/or abandoning of worldly possessions, after which they disappear off stage right, having been admitted to heaven. Some of course may be turned away and sent dismissively to the other place. Year numbers are called during this process. HEAD ANGEL speaks mostly in Spanish, which is translated by TRANSLATOR ANGEL; of course s/he can speak perfectly idiomatic English when s/he wants to. The TRANSLATOR ANGEL often virtually anticipates HEAD ANGEL.

HEAD ANGEL: (*Spanish, to Audience.*) Mil novecientos cuarenta y tre?

TRANSLATOR: 1943 (*No-one responds.*)

HEAD ANGEL: 1943, nacido en 1907?

TRANSLATOR: 1943, born in 1907?

ANGEL 1 nudges MARTIN.

ANGEL 1: It's your turn.

MARTIN, puzzled but co-operative, goes up to the desk, where are seated HEAD ANGEL and CHARLIE.

CHARLIE: Good evening.

MARTIN: Hello.

HEAD ANGEL: 1943?

MARTIN: Apparently.

HEAD ANGEL: Por favor, tome asiento.

TRANSLATOR: Do sit down.

MARTIN: Thank you.

Compressed soundtrack of MAJOR MARTIN's whole life plays, especially the elements we will see during the latter part of the play, while the officials/angels sort him out.

HEAD ANGEL: Son solo unas formalidades – nada muy complicado.

TRANSLATOR: Just a few formalities, nothing too complicated.

HEAD ANGEL: Podría poner sus cosas aquí.

TRANSLATOR: Could you put your bag there, please?

He does. HEAD ANGEL and CHARLIE start going through the stuff in transparent plastic bag, HEAD ANGEL listing it out loud and CHARLIE noting it on typewriter. ANGEL 1 arrives with cuppa.

ANGEL 1: Nice cup of tea for you Major.

MARTIN: Oh – thank you…

ANGEL 1: Milk and sugar, Major?

MARTIN: Yes, please – I'm a little bit…woozy.

HEAD ANGEL: Pasa muy seguido, es normal.

ANGEL 1: One lump or two?

MARTIN: Five please. (*Surprising self with reflex nature of the answer.*)

ANGEL 1: Terribly bad for the teeth – (*To CHARLIE.*) five sugars.

MARTIN: I feel like death warmed-up.

CHARLIE: (*Chuckles.*) Death warmed-up – very good.

ANGEL 1: Don't worry, soon be right as rain again. There we go.

MARTIN has the cuppa by now.

MARTIN: Thanks… There's nothing a nice cup of tea can't cure.

CHARLIE: I wouldn't go that far. (*To TEA ANGEL.*) Thank you Francis.

ANGEL 1: My pleasure. (*TEA ANGEL starts collecting his stuff.*)

HEAD ANGEL: Bien, solo unas preguntas,

TRANSLATOR: Now, just a few questions,

HEAD ANGEL: Y lo dejamos ir

TRANSLATOR: and we can send you on your way -

MARTIN: Is this a hospital?

HEAD ANGEL: Qué? (*Looking to CHARLIE for support.*) –

CHARLIE: Oh no, no. Sorry, you're way past that, hate to disappoint.

MARTIN: Then where am I?

CHARLIE: (*He sings.*) Dah dah dah dah. (*Tune of 'I'm in Heaven'.*)

MARTIN: Beg pardon?

CHARLIE: Dah dah dah dah.

ANGEL 1 AND ANGEL DANIEL: (*Waltzing, completing first phrases of song.*) Dah dah dah dah, dah dah dah dah, dah dah dah dah dah dah dah dah dah dah dee.

CHARLIE: Does that help?

MARTIN: This is a joke – a practical joke…isn't it?…

CHARLIE: Sadly…

CHARLIE/HEAD/OTHER ANGELS: No.

MARTIN: Shit…

CHARLIE: Oh dear.

MARTIN: This is heaven?

HEAD ANGEL: Éstrictamente hablando –

TRANSLATOR: Strictly speaking –

HEAD ANGEL: Esta seriá la antesala del cielo.

TRANSLATOR: this is the ante-room to Heaven.

CHARLIE: But you're almost there – (*DANIEL angel starts singing 'Knock Knock Knocking On Heaven's Door'.*) – we just have to check a few things.

Thank you Daniel. (*Shutting up singing actor.*)

HEAD ANGEL: No es lo que usted esperaba?

TRANSLATOR: Is it not as you expected it to be?

MARTIN: Well … I don't know.

CHARLIE: Cups of tea, Vera Lynn, It must seem very earthy.

HEAD ANGEL: Traen eso con ustedes.

TRANSLATOR: You bring that with you of course.

MARTIN: Explain.

CHARLIE: Each of you sees it in your own earthly way. Over there sits a woman who hears Tibetan nose-chants and the swish of azure prairie grasses – us she sees as orange-clad monks. That fellow there (*Pointing.*) experiences this as an abstract canvas by the artist Mark Rothko.

For the young man in the corner, this whole vision is underscored by a track from the popular beat combo, 'the Status Quo'… We carry our worlds with us, even into heaven.

HEAD ANGEL: Todo depende de su historia

TRANSLATOR: It all depends on your history.

MARTIN: (*Thinks.*) I am not sure I know my history.

CHARLIE: It's terrible – no-one knows any history any more…

HEAD ANGEL: No ese tipo de historia, no la historia oficial –

TRANSLATOR: Not that sort of history, not the official history –

MARTIN: That's not what I mean –

CHARLIE: And I don't think you feature much in the official history.

HEAD ANGEL: – your history, your story.

MARTIN: (*Annoyed.*) I know what history means – it's just –

HEAD ANGEL: Yes?

MARTIN: I don't know who I am.

CHARLIE: Ah! And you… (*Leans forward, lifts the cross around MARTIN's neck.*) …with your crucifix too.

HEAD ANGEL: A la mierda. (*Starts closing up record books etc.*)

TRANSLATOR: Oh dear.

Pause.

MARTIN: Have I said something wrong?

HEAD ANGEL: Conôcete a ti mismo. Know thyself.

MARTIN: Eh?

CHARLIE: Know thyself. Complete self-knowledge… It's a condition of entry.

MARTIN: Really? But I've obviously done something right… otherwise I wouldn't be here, would I? I'd be in the other place.

CHARLIE: They do occasionally make mistakes –

HEAD ANGEL: I am afraid it's not enough just to have washed up here – you need to know your story –

MAJOR MARTIN tries to remember.

VOICE OF CHURCHILL: And if it doesn't work, you'll just have to toss him back in the water…

MARTIN: (*Startled.*) What I do remember – is just a rush of things. It doesn't make sense…

CHURCHILL: You'll just have to toss him back in the water.

MARTIN: Couldn't you just tell me?

HEAD ANGEL: Hay gente esperando

TRANSLATOR: There are other people waiting.

CHURCHILL: Toss him back in the water, and try again.

MARTIN: You must know –

HEAD ANGEL: Ese no es el punto

TRANSLATOR: That is not the point.

HEAD ANGEL: No estamos aquí para informárle, es usted quien tiene acordarse

TRANSLATOR: It is not for us to tell but for you to remember.

MARTIN: I …

CHARLIE: Look at your things… What you have will help you work out who you are.

MARTIN, still confused, looks at his things.

HEAD ANGEL: Rápido por favor. Lo que tiene, le va ayudar entender quien es usted

TRANSLATOR: Quickly, please. What you have will help you work out who you are.

VOICE: You are what you have.

MARTIN: Cigarettes. Money. Bills…… Gun.

CHARLIE: Very impressive…there's usually a card.

MARTIN: Martin – William. Captain RM.

CHARLIE: Royal Marines.

MARTIN: Acting Major. Major William Martin. Royal Marines. There's a photo. Is this me? (*Hands photo to CHARLIE – identity card is projected for audience.*)

CHARLIE: Dead in the war. (*Hands photo back to MARTIN, who looks blank.*) The second war, that is.

MARTIN: Oh.

CHARLIE: It's quite normal not to recognise oneself – and you would have been taller in life –

HEAD ANGEL: Look in the top pocket of your uniform. There is a letter and another photo. A little wet perhaps. Now read the letter.

MARTIN: (*He finds letter and reads.*) 'My darling William. The bloodhound has left his kennel for half-an-hour so here I am scribbling nonsense to you again…your letter came this morning, just as I was dashing out…madly late as usual…why did we go and meet in the middle of a…love and kisses from Pam.' Pam?

SCENE 3B

The actress who plays the writer of the letter takes over.

MISS BOXALL: You do write such heavenly letters. But what are these horrible dark hints you're throwing out about being sent off somewhere – of course I won't say a word to anyone – I never do when you tell me things, but it's not abroad is it? Because I won't have it, I WON'T, tell them so from me… – if it weren't for the war, we might have been nearly married by now. I'm so thrilled with my ring – scandalously extravagant – you know how I adore diamonds – And I simply can't stop looking at it… Look, darling, I've got next Sunday and Monday off. I shall go home for it of course, do come if you possibly can – and see your Pam…

HEAD ANGEL: Vale?

TRANSLATOR: Well.

Black and white film projection of pretty girl in bathing costume playing at seaside.

MISS BOXALL: Do come if you possibly can or even if you can't get away from London I'll dash up and we'll have an evening of gaiety… Here comes the Bloodhound, masses of love and kisses, from Pam.

HEAD ANGEL: Vale?

MARTIN: I am a Major, I am going abroad, I am in love with Pam and she is in love with me – I have been in the wars.

Pause.

HEAD ANGEL: Good try my friend, but not quite good enough.

MARTIN: But –

HEAD ANGEL: (*Wrapping up.*) Tienen las usuales venti-quatro horas celestials abajo en las ruinas.

TRANSLATOR: You have the usual twenty-four heavenly hours back down in the ruins.

HEAD ANGEL: (*To CHARLIE.*) Lléven-lo a cualquier lugar donde se lo podría dar ayuda.

TRANSLATOR: He is telling him to take you anywhere that might help…

CHARLIE packing up stuff, closing station.

MARTIN: Hold on, isn't there anyone else I could see?

HEAD ANGEL: Y se para ese entonces no se acuerda

TRANSLATOR: And if he hasn't got it by then,

HEAD ANGEL: Me temo que es adiós Vera Lynn, hola Elvis Presley

TRANSLATOR: I'm afraid its bye bye Vera Lynn, hello Elvis Presley.

CHARLIE: I like Elvis Presley.

HEAD ANGEL: La música del Diablo.

TRANSLATOR: The Devil's music.

HEAD ANGEL: À toute à l'heure. (*She goes.*)

MARTIN: Elvis who?

CHARLIE: Don't worry your head about it – another time, another place – all time is jumbled up here –

MARTIN: Who am I?

CHARLIE: Start by looking in the mirror. Do you like what you see?

He hands him a mirror. MARTIN looks in it.

MARTIN: I do not remember.

CHARLIE: You're an enigma.

MARTIN: Enigma.

VOICEOVER: Mincemeat.

MARTIN: Mincemeat? (*Sound/LFX starts, furniture is moved, stage changes, people appear.*)

What's happening?

CHARLIE: We're going on a journey, back.

MARTIN: To earth?

CHARLIE: Not exactly – we'll be in a sort of limbo, where the memories are archived.

MARTIN: And I will find out who…

CHARLIE: You may do – and then again you may never know – not everything you see will be reliable, it's difficult to get to the bottom of things…

MARTIN: And you will help me?

CHARLIE: I will help you and all the staff of the organisation will do their best to help you fill in the blanks – won't you lads?

ALL: yes etc./sure thing/yes sah/etc

CHARLIE: London 1943 –

5: What class?

CHARLIE: Upper Echelons and Lower Depths.

The company again briefly practise the posh voice exercises, and working-class voice exercises.

CHARLIE: Let's go.

SCENE 4A

Same setting, actors change set and switch into story-telling.

2: A history lesson:

1: We are in the throes of the Second World War –

4: The War is on the turn, the Nazis –

6: (*Churchill voice, correction.*) The Narzies.

4: The Narzies have made the big mistake of abandoning their immediate intention to invade Britain, turning instead towards Russia, and here they are now bogged down, terribly.

Newspaper arrives with CHARLIE.

4/8: In the nick of time, the Blitz having wrought havoc on the lives of Londoners, rendering many thousands homeless, that nightly terror is over, and till the V1s and V2s start coming, London can rest easy.

CHARLIE: Let's start by looking in the paper – that's always a good source of information…the *Times* of June 4th 1943 reports your death – (*He reads.*) killed 'meeting the general hazards of war, next of kin have been notified', just below the death of Leslie Howard.

MARTIN: Leslie Who?

CHARLIE: (*Reading/scanning.*) Leslie Howard, VIP – shot down in a plane over Lisbon –apparently a case of mistaken identity – a local spy saw a man with a cigar board a plane, and thought it was Churchill.

MARTIN: I'd quite like to get on with my search, I only have a limited time.

CHARLIE: Just a moment, this is very interesting – he'll probably be up here soon, I need to be briefed. (*Reads.*) Leslie Howard born Leslie Stainer, took up acting as a therapy, when invalided out of the first world war. (*Looks up.*) Is acting therapeutic?

ALL: (*Hyper-relaxed.*) Oh, yes…….

MARTIN: Well that's all very well, but –

CHARLIE: Wait – I have an obituary, I don't know where it appeared –

ACTOR: (*In* Times *obituary mode.*) Bill Martin's death 'on active service' came as a complete surprise to many of his friends. Few of them knew that he had for some time been serving with the Commandos where hitherto unsuspected qualities had been revealed. (*Beat.*) Martin was a unique personality and his loss is tragic. An ever growing number of his more discerning contemporaries were convinced that he had genius.

MARTIN: I had genius – I say!

CHARLIE: (*Scanning.*) 'A happy childhood spent at Charterhouse… (*Skipping.*) school…athletics…music. After a university career during which he impressed with his literary talents and qualities of leadership…he retired into the country to farm, fish and write.'

OBIT: On the outbreak of the War, Martin hastened to offer his services to his country. Placed at first in an office job, his efforts to escape into more active and dangerous work were ultimately successful.

MARTIN: I could have continued my pleasant rural life, writing, but I felt I had to give something to my country – something dangerous.

CHARLIE: I say, well done, you sound important, you were brave, you certainly 'made a difference'.

MARTIN: Made a difference.

CHARLIE: It's a thing people will say in the next century.

MARTIN: About me?

CHARLIE: Maybe…

MARTIN: But what did I actually do, that is the question…I remember something. I am in the water, it is warm, warm water, not like Barry Island…

SCENE 4B

The sea at night. Sounds and images.

MARTIN: What do I call you?

CHARLIE: Whatever you like. Whatever you see in my face. It doesn't matter.

MAJOR MARTIN peers at him.

MARTIN: Charlie, then.

CHARLIE: What?

MARTIN: The way you look. – Charlie Chaplin.

Sound of the engine of a submarine.

CHARLIE: Hush.

We hear the voice of the submarine commander, Lieutenant Jewell, from the burial at sea scene – as if emerging from static.

VOICE OF JEWELL: Lift him out. Carefully. Carefully. Unwrap the blanket.

MARTIN: What is this?

CHARLIE: Hush.

VOICE OF JEWELL: Harris, don't look if it upsets you. Inflate his Mae West. Are we steady?

OFFICER 4: Steady sir.

Sea sounds and electronic interference noise, get louder.

MARTIN: I can't hear what they're saying.

CHARLIE: Wait.

The voices fade back in.

VOICE OF JEWELL: Let him go… Is he floating?

OFFICER 4: Yes sir.

VOICE OF JEWELL: Towards the land?

OFFICER 4: Towards the land sir, he'll be in Spain soon.

MARTIN: Spain – I feel like I always wanted to go to Spain – tell me about Spain, was Spain on our side?

CHARLIE: Spain: theoretically neutral in World War Two, recovering from its own savage civil war when General Franco took over to crush a short-lived democratic republic, resulting in one of the few wars to feature anarchist militias (along with bags of socialists who came from all over the world including Britain to show solidarity with the Spanish left). Franco had won by this point, with a little help from Hitler – so not really as neutral as it might have been.

SCENE 4C

The sea, fishing boats, Huelva in Spain, fishermen, early in the morning. A scene in Spanish and German, most of which is dubbed by two actors voicing the scene seated at microphone table, while other actors perform it and mouth when speaking. And sometimes the actors themselves are speaking. There is a touch of the 'Allo 'Allo about it all.

Ethereal movement fishing sequence with sea shore sounds. We see fishermen fishing. Many. We see one pair catch a body, and bring it to the shore. We see the crowd around it. The body has an attaché case attached by a chain to the wrist. We see Spanish informer going off to German consulate.

SPANISH INFORMER: (*At door of GERMAN CONSULATE.*) Hay un cadaver de un soldado en la playa y tiene un maletín. (*Demonstrating the attaché case.*) [There is the body of a soldier on the beach and it is holding an attaché case.]

GERMAN OFFICIAL: Espere aquí. [Wait here.]

OFFICIAL goes to GERMAN CONSUL, who is Germanically engaged.

Enschuldigen-Sie, Herr Konsul, da ist ein man hier der sagt dass am Strand die Leiche eines Britischen Soldaten mit ein Aktentasche liegt. [Excuse me, Sir, there is a man here who says that on the beach there is lying the body of a British soldier with an attaché case.]

CONSUL: Sagen sie ihm dass er die Aktentasche hier zum Konsulat bringen soll. Schnell. [Tell him to bring the attaché case to the consulate. Quickly.]

OFFICIAL returns to INFORMER at door.

GERMAN OFFICIAL: Traelo aquí. Rapido. [Bring it here. Quickly.]

SPANISH INFORMER: Si Senõr. [Yes sir.]

He sets off to bring the briefcase to the consulate. At the same time, another SPANIARD is visiting the BRITISH CONSULATE.

OTHER SPANIARD: Hay un cadaver en la playa, parece uno de los suyos y tiene un maletín. [There is a corpse on the beach, looks like one of yours and its got an attaché case.]

BRITISH OFFICIAL: Espere aquí. [Wait here.]

He goes to BRITISH CONSUL who is taking tea.

(*Coughs to alert CONSUL.*) Excuse me sir, but there is a man here who says they've found a body on the beach, one of ours apparently, with an attaché case.

BRITISH CONSUL: An attaché case – I see – tell the man to bring the body here.

BRITISH OFFICIAL: (*To SPANIARD.*) Traelo aquí. [Bring it here.]

BRITISH CONSUL: Quick as you can old chap.

OTHER SPANIARD: Si Señor. [Yes sir.]

The SPANISH INFORMER has got the briefcase to the Germans, who are now perusing its contents, and taking photos. We see projections of these contents which include a number of letters.

GERMAN CONSUL: (*To GERMAN OFFICIAL, translating from letters.*) Wenn Major Martin züruck-kommt, konnt er einige Sardinen mit-bringen, sie sind hier rationiert. [When Major Martin comes back, could he bring some Sardines with him, they are rationed here.]

GERMAN OFFICIAL: (*Getting the reference.*) Haw haw haw – Sardinen – Haw haw haw – Sardinen. [Ha ha ha – Sardines Ha ha ha – Sardines.]

GERMAN CONSUL: Sardinen – Sardinien. [Sardines – Sardinia.]

The OTHER SPANIARD brings the body to the British.

BRITISH OFFICIAL: (*Coughs to alert CONSUL.*)

BRITISH CONSUL: Very good – but where's the attaché case old chap, where's the attaché case?

BRITISH OFFICIAL: (*To other SPANIARD.*) É ! Donde está el maletín ? [where is the case?]

OTHER SPANIARD: No lo se – me he dormindo. [I don't know – I was sleeping.]

BRITISH OFFICIAL: Ve te de aquí, gilipollas. [Get out of here, asshole.]

OTHER SPANIARD leaves. The Germans are still doubled up with laughter about the sardines joke.

GERMAN OFFICIAL: Haw haw haw – Sardinen. [Ha ha ha – Sardines.]

As the OTHER SPANIARD leaves the BRITISH CONSULATE, the SPANISH INFORMER arrives there with the attaché case.

SPANISH INFORMER: (*Coughs to alert BRITISH CONSUL.*)

GERMAN CONSUL: Sardinen – Sardinien. [Sardines – Sardinia.]

SPANISH INFORMER: Es esto lo que estabais buscando ? [Is this what you have been looking for?]

BRITISH CONSUL: Has anyone opened this?

BRITISH OFFICIAL: Alguem lo a abierto?

SPANISH INFORMER: No.

BRITISH CONSUL: Very good – here's something for your trouble.

This scene fades into background as CONSUL takes possession of case.

MARTIN: I was some kind of secret agent – I was clearly carrying important papers, which the Germans were keen to photograph – something to do with Sardines, I think.

CHARLIE: Yes…

MARTIN: But as luck would have it, I managed to find myself in a plane crash, so my mission was clearly not successful – if I was a courier, my messages ended up with the wrong people – not such a brilliant career after all.

CHARLIE: You may be being hard on yourself.

MARTIN: I was loved once, by 'Pem' (*He imitates her accent.*) – but why do I not remember her – and why would I end up in Heaven if I am such an unsuccessful or inept secret agent? I'd've thought my colleagues in the Marines would be fuming…

SCENE 4D

CHARLIE: Let's go back a bit further – to the Admiralty before your plane took off. Secret Agent Major Martin, see if you recognise any fellow Marines.

A group of men round a table, looking at photographs of young women which one of them is projecting onto a screen. This is the Twenty Committee, responsible for deception operations in WW2. Amongst them CHARLES CHOLMONDLEY and a young EWEN MONTAGU, chief architects of Operation Mincemeat. CHOLMONDLEY stays in shadows throughout. Photo of first young woman.

OFFFICER 1: What ho!

OFFICER 2: Cha cha cha.

OFFICER 3: Well hello.

CHOLMONDLEY: I say – she's a bit of a looker, Montagu.

MONTAGU: Not my type.

New picture.

No – I don't think so.

New picture.

ALL MALES: (*Chorus.*) NO!

New picture.

CHOMONDLEY: No.

MONTAGU: Maybe –

OFFICER 3: Bit well-built on top.

OFFICER 2: Ooh la la.

New picture.

CHOLMONDLEY: What about her?

MONTAGU: (*Deciding immediately.*) That's Pam – that's my Pam.

OFFICER 3: Oh – I like her. She's a bit of alright.

OFFICER 2: Ding dong.

MONTAGU: I reckon Major Martin would like her. Who is she?

CHOLMONDLEY: Who do you want her to be?

OFFICER 3: The mother of his children –

OFFICER 1: The perfect wife.

OFFICER 2: Choo choo choo.

CHOLMONDLEY: She's Lucy – Lucy something – one of the girls from the map-room –

MONTAGU: She'll do.

MARTIN: She's not Lucy – she's Pam, she's my Pam, don't they know her?

CHOLMONDLEY: I'll tell her the good news that we've fixed her up with a Major.

OFFICER 3: I'm sure she'll be delighted.

SCENE 4E

We switch to the secretarial pool, where MISS BOXALL, AGNES (played by a man) and MARIA are working on the production of convincing love-letters – in suitably fun, giggly but dedicated style. They have cut-glass 1950s accents, as do all the men earlier.

MISS BOXALL: Alright – mine's a girl of about twenty. Very well brought up. Works in an office perhaps, much like ours, with a dreary boss,

AGNES/MARIA: much like ours –

MISS B: and she's writing the letter when she should really be doing something more serious. Agnes?

AGNES: Mine's a thoughtful left-leaning woman, a member of Mass Observation and the Left Book club, telling her fiancé how things really are at home.

MISS B: I've a feeling Commander Montagu wanted something rather more domesticated…a bit more fluttery…

AGNES: Damn what Montagu wanted... I am a passionate woman writing to my man – I will not be tamed.

MISS B: Of course not. Maria, what have you done?

MARIA: (*She is Spanish.*) I started off with a foreign girl, an alien who had been interned at the start of the war as a potential fifth columnist.

AGNES: Now who could that be based on?

MARIA: But I gave up halfway through –

AGNES/MISS B: Why?

MARIA: She started turning into a lesbian. (*Giggles.*)

MISS B: I don't think Montagu and co are quite ready for lesbians yet – read a bit of yours Agnes.

AGNES: (*She reads.*) 'Dear William – I am writing to you not from Hampstead but from a cramped but comfortable shelter in Tilbury in the East End of London. I was helping out at a reception centre for the newly homeless when the sirens went, and off we all trooped, very calmly, past the bombed out houses and down to the shelter. I dare say your life is much more exciting than mine, what with your foreign assignments and such –'

MARIA: Montagu wanted us to mention that –

AGNES: 'But I have to say that this is the most exciting time of my life. It's so good to be useful, to be doing more than just making tea. Some people are actually living down here, mostly poor people, but they're ever so friendly if you give them a chance. This shelter is not like other places I've been – they have their own rules and everything, they have even published their own newspaper.. Everyone is talking about how things will be different after the war, when we get socialism. Oh dear, someone needs my help – more later – love Agnes.' What do you think?

MISS B: She's a wonder but they wouldn't quite see her point of view.

MARIA: I think they would prefer my lesbian.

AGNES: Really? Oh dear...

MARIA: Patricia – you are our last hope.

MISS B: 'My darling William. The bloodhound has left his kennel for half an hour so here I am scribbling nonsense to you again. Your letter came this morning just as I was dashing out – madly late as usual.'

AGNES: 'Madly late' – that's perfect.

MISS B: 'You do write such heavenly letters. But what are these horrible dark hints you're throwing out about being sent off somewhere – it's not abroad is it? Because I won't have it, I WON'T, tell them so from me.' Is that fluttery enough?

AGNES: She's going to take off any minute. Who's the lucky man anyway?

MARIA: Montagu wouldn't tell us.

AGNES: Well, I hope he's worth it. Go on Patricia – the men will love it.

MISS B reads on, with ever-increasing passion

The scene and MAJOR MARTIN's process of deduction are simultaneous.

MISS B: 'Darling – why did we go and meet in the middle of a war, such a silly thing for anyone to do – if it weren't for the war, we might have been nearly married by now. I'm so thrilled with my ring – scandalously extravagant – you know how I adore diamonds – And I simply

MAJOR MARTIN: I am going under cover and they are giving me a fictional identity.

CHARLIE: Now we are getting somewhere...

MAJOR MARTIN: Pam is not my real fiancée – she doesn't exist.

can't stop looking at it. Look, darling, I've got next Sunday and Monday off. I shall go home for it of course, do come if you possibly can …' Where's the other piece of paper?

'Or even if you can't get away from London I'll dash up and we'll have an evening of gaiety… Here comes the Bloodhound. Masses of love and kisses, from Pam.'

Pam is a girl who works in my office.

CHARLIE: She's vanished, old chap, nice while it lasted.

MAJOR MARTIN: And this Montagu person is clearly my boss – he's the one in charge.

MARIA: Pam. She'll do anything for him, won't she?

AGNES: I can imagine what he's like. Lots of fizz.

MARIA: It's good, it's very good. Where do you get it all from?

MISS B: I have lived Maria, I have lived.

MARIA: Let's hope Montagu and Cholmondley like it.

AGNES: They're in seventh heaven right now, staring at naughty pictures of us and choosing…

Laughter. Exeunt.

CHARLIE: Very very good – no wonder you fancy yourself as a secret agent – you are like Sherlock Holmes.

MARTIN: Elementary my dear Charlie.I have genius, (*Reminding him of the obituary.*) Charlie, I have genius. Right – well, we just need to tie up the loose ends, and then we can get back to the heaven formalities, I feel ready to go in now.

CHARLIE: Not quite I'm afraid – there's more…

MARTIN: More?

CHARLIE: Let's see Commander Montagu and his team in the cold light of a morning.

SCENE 4F

*The Twenty Committee meeting again. SECRETARY MAUD corrects
MONTAGU's frequent mistakes. Whenever MONTAGU mentions
CHOLMONDLEY's name (which is pronounced Chumley),
CHOLMONDLEY coughs to cover it up.*

MAUD: (*Going round.*) Can everyone in Section 12 gather in
the briefing room, Commander Montagu is going to share
some pearls of wisdom with us.

MONTAGU: Squadron Leader Cholmondley and I have been
up all night working on Mincemeat, so forgive me if I am
less than completely coherent. As you know, Mr Churchill
is of the opinion that, 'anybody but a damned fool will
know' that the opening of our second front in Europe,
after the success of our North African campaigns, will be
launched with the invasion of Sardinia.

MAUD: Sicily.

MONTAGU: Sorry, with the invasion of Sicily – the 'soft
underbelly of Europe'.

MAUD: As Mr Churchill would have it.

MONTAGU: Thank you Marjorie – our task in Deception, is to
make the Boche think that we are going somewhere else
– like maybe Sicily.

MAUDI: Sardinia.

MONTAGU: My God I'm tired – Sardinia – or Greece… Millie,
could you get me a coffee…let me start again – I seem to
have confused myself… We want to make Jerry think that
we are not coming through Sicily, but landing instead on
Sardinia and Greece.

MAUD: Well done sir.

MONTAGU: Thank you Maggie. Cholmondley here had an
idea –

MONTAGU stuffs a pipe, CHARLIE and MAJOR MARTIN whisper.

MARTIN: Who's this Cholmondley he keeps talking about?

CHARLIE: Cholmondley is a spook.

MARTIN: A ghost?

CHARLIE: Sort of – a career secret agent, not a temporary one like Mr Montagu – a rather shadowy figure, stays out of the limelight – so we never see Cholmondley in full light or without a disguise. Even his name is not spelt as it sounds.

MARTIN: That is spooky.

MONTAGU: Cholmondley here had an idea, to deceive the Boche. We have drafted up some letters between high level commanders designed to fall into the hands of the Boche – Monica.

MAUD: A letter from General Nye to General Alexander in North Africa, a letter from General Mountbatten to General Eisenhower, and one letter from General Mountbatten to the Admiral of the Fleet.

MONTAGU: These letters craftily let slip careless references to the fact that we are not going for Sicily after all – including a little joke designed to appeal to the Teutonic idea of British humour, which will make the Boche think it might be Sardinia – Meredith?

MAUD hands him letter.

(*Reading.*) 'I say, I bet SARDINES are difficult to get hold of there…'

ALL: Arf arf.

AGNES: The letter Sir. (*Retrieving it.*)

MONTAGU: Then we make sure that the Boche get hold of these letters – this is where Major Martin comes in…he will carry these letters and deliver them to Spain, where we can be sure a less-than-neutral Spaniard will convey them to Jerry.

I have been to the very highest level to gain clearance for this operation – Uncle John.

CHARLIE: That's Johny Bevan, Montagu's boss.

MONTAGU: Uncle John has been to see the old man himself.

MARTIN: Churchill – Churchill knew about my mission?

CHURCHILL speech voiceover. Then Actor appears becoming CHURCHILL.

CHURCHILL ACTOR: Brandy please. Cigar. Papers. (*These are supplied.*)

Get me Roosevelt. Get me Stalin. Get me Beaverbrook. This is my finest hour. Blood, sweat and tears.

S/he casts fellow actors as necessary.

Now – you're Montagu's boss Johny Bevan, they've let you in. And you're my – personal secretary. You just fuss around me and you – you come up to me, come on.

JOHNY BEVAN: Sir, Prime Minister.

CHURCHILL: Who the blazes are you?

PERSONAL SEC: It's Bevan sir. The Admiralty.

CHURCHILL: Well?

JOHNY BEVAN: It's about Mincemeat sir.

CHURCHILL: Mincemeat? Mincemeat?

PERSONAL SEC: Invasion of Sicily sir, deception plans.

CHURCHILL: Ah Mincemeat – yes, why didn't you say so – the corpse who speaks. What about him?

MARTIN: Corpse?

JOHNY BEVAN: We're ready to go sir. Everything's in place.

CHURCHILL: Good, good. So you're going to persuade them it's not Sicily when any bloody fool can look at the map and see that it's got to be Sicily.

JOHNY BEVAN: Yes sir.

CHURCHILL: You're some kind of deception wizard are you?

JOHNY BEVAN: No sir. But we think we've got the right man for the job.

CHURCHILL: Well you'd better throw him in then. Give him a chance.

JOHNY BEVAN: Yes sir. Thank you. (*He starts to leave.*)

CHURCHILL: And Bevan…

JOHNY BEVAN: Yes sir.

CHURCHILL: If it doesn't work this time, you'll just have to throw him in again won't you?

JOHNY BEVAN: Yes sir, until we get it right.

CHURCHILL: Good show. (*S/he takes a big swig of brandy.*) Make it lifelike. Good show.

SCENE 4G

Back to meeting and MAJOR MARTIN and CHARLIE's observation.

MARTIN: Corpse? – they meant for me to get drowned.

AGNES: I have Sir Bernard Spilsbury for you Commander.

MONTAGU: Spilsbury?

AGNES: The pathologist, Sir – you wanted to know about causes of death and visible symptoms.

MONTAGU: Of course – Hello?

SPILSBURY BY PHONE: Hello?

MONTAGU: Hello?

SPILSBURY: Hello?

MONTAGU: Hello?

SPILSBURY: Hello?

MONTAGU: Hello. Spilsbury, good to hear you old chap.

CHARLIE: (*Whispers.*) Bernard Spilsbury, the founding father of forensic science in this country.

SPILSBURY: Don't have much time, research to be done – the short answer to your question is – there is not a pathologist in Spain skilled enough to tell the difference between phosphorus poisoning and death by drowning after a fall from a plane – need any help, speak to Bentley Purchase, coroner at St Pancras – he should be able to sort you out.

MARTIN: Phosphorus? That's what they use to kill rats… Was I poisoned?

CHARLIE: Poisoning was the cause of your death.

MARTIN: (*Dawning horror.*) They poisoned me.

CHARLIE: Steady now, you're getting paranoid…

MARTIN: I don't believe it…my own people, fellow navy officers poisoned me and dropped me in the sea off the coast of Spain…

CHARLIE: You know I am not allowed to comment.

MARTIN: Good God – it's hard to credit… I mean if it was that important, why did they not just approach me…ask me… this is Major William Martin speaking… Bill Martin…I have genius… I might have said yes…but to poison me…

CHARLIE: *Dulce et decorum est pro patria mori.*

MARTIN: Eh?

CHARLIE: It is a sweet and fitting thing to die for one's country.

MARTIN: Is it?

CHARLIE: Better than just keeling over in the street one day…

MARTIN: (*Half a memory.*) Somehow I think I've already done my fair share of keeling over…

CHARLIE: You see, you are starting to remember things, well done… He's starting to remember things, everyone, well done, keep up the good work.

ALL: Thank God for that/Phew/etc.

MARTIN: I am to die, but in death I am to be entrusted with this very important errand – under cover…through my sacrifice, thousands of lives will be saved…

CHARLIE: On the right lines Major, but still not quite there. Let's go down. (*To audience.*) By all means follow us, I'm afraid the office is closed for the rest of the heavenly day.

The audience is processed to next space. In fact the space they started in, by a different route. When they arrive there, there is a strange container, a human-sized cylinder, like a mini-submarine, on chocks in the middle of the space.

SCENE 5A

The warehouse. In the middle of the stage: the container. LIEUTENANT JEWEL, submarine commander, alone with voice of EWEN MONTAGU.

MONTAGU'S RECORDED VOICE : Two skins of 22-gauge sheet steel welded together. Asbestos wool between the skins. The lid airtight with sixteen nuts. At either end a lifting handle. Total weight: empty – 250 pounds; full – about 400.

This container will contain a body. Packed around with dry ice to prevent decomposition. This body is to be transported, in the submarine HMS Seraph, to Spanish waters, as near as prudently possible to the mouth of the river Huelva. There the container is to be opened and the body deposited in the water, in such a way that it is borne by the tides and prevailing winds to land. Can you do that, Lieutenant Jewell?

JEWELL: If your information about the tides and prevailing winds is accurate.

VOICE OF MONTAGU: To the best of our knowledge.

CHARLIE: Full fathom five thy father lies – those are pearls that were his eyes.

JEWELL: Tell me the details.

VOICE OF MONTAGU: Operation Mincemeat: 'Object. To cause a briefcase containing documents to drift ashore as near as possible to Huelva in Spain in such circumstances that it will be thought to have been washed ashore from an aircraft which crashed at sea when the case was being taken by an officer from Britain to Allied Forces HQ in North Africa.'

CHARLIE: Full fathom five…

VOICE OF MONTAGU: Body and briefcase to be delivered separately to the commander of the submarine, 'When the body is removed from the container all that will be necessary will be to fasten the chain attached to the briefcase through the belt of the trench-coat worn by the body…body then to be deposited in the water, along with rubber dinghy, which should float separately, near, but not too near, the body.'

JEWELL: What should I tell the crew?

MONTAGU: Tell them they are carrying a secret weather-reporting device. Once the body is in the sea, you'll have to tell them something different.

JEWELL: And if things go wrong?

MONTAGU: If the operation has to be cancelled a signal will be made – 'Cancel Mincemeat'. In which case the body and container are to be sunk in deep water. While the briefcase should be handed to the Staff Officer, Intelligence at Gibraltar, with instructions to burn the contents unopened.

JEWELL: So the briefcase is the important thing.

VOICE OF MONTAGU: Yes.

JEWELL: More than the body?

VOICE OF MONTAGU: The body is the key to the whole operation. Without the body, the contents of the briefcase will not possess credibility. With the body, they become persuasive. The body, you might say, vouches for them. He is their referee.

JEWELL: I see.

VOICE OF MONTAGU: Any questions, Lieutenant Jewell?

Pause.

JEWELL: When do I sail?

VOICE OF MONTAGU: Very soon. I take delivery of the body tonight.

Exit JEWELL.

SCENE 5B

MARTIN: I'm dead already aren't I? By this time I'm dead already.

CHARLIE: So it would seem.

MARTIN: Did they kill me?

CHARLIE: No way of knowing I'm afraid, Major, depends how desperate you think they were –

MARTIN: Stop calling me Major – I'm not a Major am I?

CHARLIE: You certainly weren't a Major till they gave you this job.

MARTIN: Maybe I don't even exist? Maybe I'm a complete fiction. They just made me up. I am a character in a film or something, this is all an elaborate piece of story-telling.

CHARLIE: That's an interesting idea, which may, in its way, be true – but in this case, it is also true that you are a real person, just –

MARTIN: If I am not Major Martin... I can't be nobody... I must be someone else...who am I?

CHARLIE: Let's find someone who saw you, someone real, someone so flesh and blood that no-one would make him up...

Wall projection of short film of IVOR LEVERTON, a North London undertaker, a real person speaking to camera in the year 2000, talking about picking up the body at the dead of night and delivering it to Hackney mortuary.

IVOR LEV: My family have been funeral directors for eight generations now but I never intended to be one myself. But fate, the war, and the blitz changed me in my plans.

CHARLIE: Introduce yourself.

IVOR LEV: My name is Ivor Leverton and I am probably the only person alive that saw the body.

MARTIN: What happened?

IVOR LEV: I had a call from the coroner's office, Glyn May, he worked for Bentley Purchase the coroner. I was told that I was under the Official Secrets Act, secondly I was told there were to be no records kept and nobody was to know anything about it, not even my family, thirdly, we weren't going to be paid a penny.

I alone had to be at St Pancras mortuary, one a.m., with a hearse and a coffin. I turned up at the mortuary, there was

Glyn May waiting for me, and no mortuary keeper there. So then the two of us managed to put him in the coffin and the coffin in the hearse and off we went to Hackney through deserted streets.

CHARLIE: Sounds easy – actually they could hardly get him into the coffin.

IVOR LEV: Yes – we were able by a slight bending of the knees although that was not easy because of the freezing.

Of course this was just an unknown person that we had been asked to move for the coroner, I had no idea who he was.

MARTIN: Then what happened?

IVOR LEV: Well I suppose it was about 2 o'clock by the time I got back again. Course I had to take back the removal coffin, put it into its normal place, lock up, without disturbing our people sleeping above.

MARTIN: So no one ever knew?

IVOR LEV: I think possibly our driver when he came in the next morning might have found one vehicle still with a slightly warm engine. I never asked him.

MARTIN: They must have told you his name?

IVOR LEV: I never knew who the man was – I sometimes wondered.

MARTIN: Put me out of my misery, tell me the truth, what happened to me, who am I?

CHARLIE: You are bored of the riddling? You want to know it all?

MARTIN: I can't stand this not knowing who I am – I need to know.

CHARLIE: What if you don't like who you are?

MARTIN: That's a risk I'll have to take.

CHARLIE: (*To audience.*) This way –

SCENE 6A

A mortuary. White tiles, buckets, long rubber gloves, sounds.

Audience enter the mortuary from one end, as do MAJOR MARTIN and CHARLIE – when audience are settled. CHOLMONDLEY and MONTAGU are outside, hammering on the door. FRED SHRIEVE, mortuary attendant, enters.

SHRIEVE: We're closed.

Knocking continues.

MONTAGU: Open up.

Knocking.

SHRIEVE: We're not open.

More knocking.

MONTAGU: (*Sounding aristocatic.*) Come on, open up. Do I have to get Bentley Purchase onto you? Open the door.

SHRIEVE grudgingly approaches the door.

SHRIEVE: All right. Coming.

Opens door. MONTAGU steps inside, followed by CHOLMONDLEY. They have bags with them for the clothes and for the contents of the pockets, and the briefcase.

MONTAGU: Lieutenant-Commander Montagu. Squadron Leader Cholmondley. (*CHOLMONDLEY coughs to cover up the mention of his name.*)

(*To CHOLMONDLEY.*) Sorry Charles. (*To SHRIEVE.*) As Mr Purchase warned you, everything that happens now is to be forgotten and, as specified under the terms of the Official Secrets Act, never spoken of again.

SHRIEVE: Yes?

MONTAGU: You've got a body for us, in cold storage.

SHRIEVE: Geezer with a funny name?

MONTAGU: Probably. Will you get it out for us?

SHRIEVE: I was on my way home.

MONTAGU: Just do it please.

SHRIEVE: Where do you want him?

MONTAGU: Here. Under the light.

SHRIEVE: He's not very pretty.

MONTAGU: That's not our main concern.

SHRIEVE: How'd he die?

MONTAGU: Pneumonia.

SHRIEVE: Doesn't look like pneumonia to me

MONTAGU: Just get him please.

SHRIEVE: Aye-aye sir. Right away.

He goes to get the body.

MONTAGU: A Mr Leverton delivered our friend from St
Pancras a couple of days ago. He and his fellows believe
it's something to do with the Free French.

CHOLMONDLEY: Yes of course.

SHRIEVE wheels in a trolley. The body is covered by a white sheet.

SHRIEVE: Here you are. Frozen stiff. Who is he?

MONTAGU: Suffice it to say, he is a nobody now, but by the
time we have finished with him, he will be a somebody.

CHOLMONDLEY: What's your name?

SHRIEVE: Fred Shrieve.

CHOLMONDLEY: Fred Shrieve, mortuary attendant.

SHRIEVE: That's right, sir. Friend of the dead.

MONTAGU: Just put him there, and then perhaps you could go with Squadron Leader Cholmondley (*CHOLMONDLEY coughs to cover mention of his name.*) and bring the container in from the van? It'll take both of you. Thank you.

Now it's just MONTAGU, with MARTIN and CHARLIE looking on. MARTIN much closer than CHARLIE. MONTAGU pauses, braces himself, and then lifts up the sheet.

Poor man. Poor man.

He empties the bag of clothes, hanging up the trench coat and battledress. The items of uniform are the same as those worn by MAJOR MARTIN. He pulls back the sheet and starts dressing the body.

SCENE 6B

MARTIN: (*Welsh.*) I had a dream I came home drunk, blind drunk, five sheets to the wind and legless and I was being undressed and caressed, by a lady, with such tenderness it broke my heart –

SHRIEVE and CHOLMONDLEY enter, having just carried the metal container seen earlier from the van to the morgue's ante-room, outside.

SHRIEVE: What the bloody hell is that thing?

CHOLMONDLEY: A new kind of missile, Mr Shrieve. We're going to catapult dead bodies into the heart of Berlin to depress the enemy.

MONTAGU: (*Reproving.*) Charles.

MARTIN: (*Realisation.*) That's me!

SHRIEVE: You're winding me up.

MONTAGU: Gentlemen, this is the King's duty on which we are engaged, your assistance would be appreciated.

MONTAGU and CHOLMONDLEY start dressing the body.

SHRIEVE: (*Noticing MONTAGU's difficulty.*) Try a dab of this, Sir.

MONTAGU: Eh.

SHRIEVE: (*Demonstrating.*) Vicks, under the nose. Tricks of the trade.

MONTAGU: Thanks very much. (*He and CHOLMONDLEY take a dab of Vicks Vapour Rub, like a small Hitler moustache.*)

They continue to dress the body, trying to deal with the trousers and boots.

SHRIEVE: You're going to get yourself in a right pickle there. Do you know how long this bloke's been dead?

MONTAGU: Yes we do. And we don't want him to get any deader. (*Struggling with the frozen feet.*)

SHRIEVE: You'll never get them boots on him.

MONTAGU: Why not?

SHRIEVE: Look at his plates –

MONTAGU: His what?

SHRIEVE: His feet. There's no give in them. Nothing.

CHOLMONDLEY: I say he's right you know, Ewen, they're frozen stiff.

MONTAGU: We can't wait till he thaws out – we'd be here all night. Apart from which it would advance his decomposition.

CHOLMONDLEY: Anyway you're not meant to de-freeze things and then re-freeze them. It's unhealthy.

MONTAGU: We're not going to eat him, Charles…

SHRIEVE: (*Returning with electric bar fire.*) Ta-dah ! (*He is met with blankness.*) Where they've got too stiff, sir, we often use an electric fire to help nature. Here.

He switches it on and rather too quickly holds it near the corpse's feet.

Like this.

MARTIN: Oh my God!

MONTAGU: Don't burn him!

SHRIEVE: It won't harm. It's a question of distance. – I told you – I'm a friend of the dead.

MONTAGU: One lives and learns.

SHRIEVE: Alright – you carry on with his clothes.

They carry on working. MONTAGU steps back while the other two carry on. It is quite hard work for all concerned.

BODY: Iesu Crist. – What the fuck do you think you are doing?

MONTAGU: Sincere apologies, my Welsh friend. What must you think of us?

BODY: I think it's a bloody liberty, that's what I think. Have you got anyone's permission to do this?

CHOLMONDLEY: Thank God there aren't any relatives to worry about – think of the fuss they'd make…

MARTIN: I've got relatives… I'm sure I've got relatives… everyone's got some relatives, if you really look for them…

BODY: Iesu Crist.

MONTAGU: Our chaps made enquiries – not too strenuously.

BODY: This takes the biscuit.

MONTAGU: What the eye doesn't see, the heart doesn't grieve over.

CHOLMONDLEY: As long as we're not going to have a crowd of grieving cousins after our blood in five years' time.

SHRIEVE: Is this strictly legal, your lordships?

MONTAGU: *Silent leges inter arma* – which means -

SHRIEVE: Everybody keep shtum.

MARTIN: Fucking liberty, that's what it means. (*More Welsh by the minute.*)

CHOLMONDLEY: More or less.

MONTAGU: The laws lie quiet when in arms.

BODY: Duw – if there was one place a poor bugger ought to get a bit of peace and quiet… No such luck.

SHRIEVE: There. Done him. Now I don't know what you want him for, but he's as good now as he'll ever look.

MONTAGU: All done I think.

SHRIEVE: There's a bit of green there though. (*Wipes mould off GLYNDWR's face.*) What do we do now?

MONTAGU: Kindly wait for us outside.

SHRIEVE: I could put on a brew if you don't mind it weak.

MONTAGU: That would be nice, thank you.

SHRIEVE goes out.

SCENE 6C

MONTAGU: We have a body, now we give him a life. We make him one of us.

He takes out of the briefcase a few bags and large envelopes. They continue to dress the body with the props.

Charles – let us work through the props… Identity disc and crucifix.

CHOLMONDLEY: Yes. Yes.

MONTAGU: Wristwatch, stopped at 8.37.

CHOLMONDLEY: OK. Let me just… (*Fastens it.*)

MONTAGU: Wallet containing money, bills, various official and personal documents. Identity card with photograph.

CHOLMONDLEY: Pam's photo. Pam's letters.

Brief extract from letters heard earlier. He reads:

'Darling – why did we go and meet in the middle of a war…'

MONTAGU: Top pocket, next to the heart.

CHOLMONDLEY: Bill from goldsmiths for Pam's engagement ring.

MONTAGU: Sad to say, Pam will never see it.

CHOLMONDLEY: Letter from Major Martin's father.

MONTAGU: Which I wrote – rather proud of the punctuality thing…

CHOLMONDLEY: Never saw the final version – may I ?

MONTAGU: Be my guest.

As CHOLMONDLEY reads, MONTAGU also speaks certain phrases he is proud of – underlined in text.

CHOLMONDLEY: 'I enclose a copy of the letter which I have written to Gwatkin of McKenna and Co, solicitors about your impending marriage. I have asked him to lunch with me at *the Carlton Grill at a quarter to one* on Wednesday 21st. I should be glad if you would make it possible to join us.. We shall not however *wait luncheon for you,* so I trust that, if you are able to come, you will make a point of being punctual.'

They may laugh together at its perfection.

MONTAGU: Now to the meat. Letter from Mountbatten to the Admiral of the Fleet. Letter to from General Nye to

General Alexander in North Africa. Letter to Eisenhower with the sardines joke.

CHOLMONDLEY: Roger. Matches, cigarettes, keys, pencil.

MONTAGU: That's it, I think. Well done. (*Shouting.*) Shrieve, you can come back in now.

SCENE 6D

SHRIEVE re-enters.

SHRIEVE: Tea up.

CHOLMONDLEY: You've forgotten the theatre tickets.

MONTAGU: So I have.

CHOLMONDLEY: Just put the stubs in… We can use these, can't we? Going away party?

MONTAGU: I suppose we could, yes. Jolly good idea.

SHRIEVE: What show are they for, sir, if you don't mind me asking?

CHOLMONDLEY: Sid Field, at the Prince of Wales.

SHRIEVE: Very funny man.

CHOLMONDLEY: Isn't he.

SHRIEVE: The Golf Routine.

They move into Sid Field routine.

CHOLMONDLEY: Tee up.

SHRIEVE: What what what?

CHOLMONDLEY: Tee up.

SHRIEVE: But I thought we were playing golf.

CHOLMONDLEY: We are.

SHRIEVE: Well what are you on about with the tea?

CHOLMONDLEY: I mean make a tee with sand.

SHRIEVE: Tee with sand – that's disgusting.

MONTAGU: All right, alright, we get the general gist.

CHOLMONDLEY: Very funny man.

MONTAGU: Tea up?

CHOLMONDLEY, MONTAGU and SHRIEVE go out to ante-room to drink their tea, leaving the BODY alone with MAJOR MARTIN and CHARLIE.

SCENE 6E

MARTIN: (*To BODY.*) Who are you?

BODY: What a thing to ask.

MARTIN: You're me, apparently.

BODY: Obviously.

MARTIN: But you don't even look like me.

BODY: I'm not feeling my best this evening – I feel like death warmed-up, see.

MARTIN: He doesn't even look like me – he's huge.

CHARLIE: I explained all that – you shrink after you die. No-one ever recognises themselves at first – its perfectly normal. Go, carpe diem, seize the moment – Tweedledum and Tweedledee will be back in a minute.

MARTIN: So who are you?

BODY: Your name is Glyndwr Michael. You are the illegitimate son of Thomas Michael, and Sarah Ann Chadwick of Aberbargoed, Glamorgan. You were born on January 4th 1909.

MARTIN: There must be more.

BODY: No, that's all there is, butt. Officially you are registered as a vagrant, an unemployed labourer, sometime attender at the St Pancras Lunacy Assessment Unit. I am the man you see on the corner of the street shouting at the traffic – spare any change please – that's who I am…who are you?.

MARTIN: A tramp…? A mad tramp kipping on the streets round St Pancras.

BODY: Are you disappointed then? Was you expecting someone else – ?

MARTIN: Of course I am bloody disappointed, of course– a few hours ago I was a secret agent, I had a fiancée, a father, meetings at the Savoy Grill, photos, value, importance – I owed money, and people didn't mind – I was a hero on a dangerous mission for the good of the nation – now look at me – (*Cries.*)

Pause.

BODY: Dangerous mission is it? I'll give you dangerous – dangerous is on the street, dangerous is living on your unhinged wits, dangerous is the East End, dangerous is being bombed day after day, burying friends and neighbours, no plush country estate to retire to, just communal shelters – that's dangerous, butt, that's heroic – you just can't see it so easy.

MARTIN: How could you let this happen to you…? How could you sink so low?

BODY: Happen to anyone couldn't it?

MARTIN: How?

BODY: There is a moment when you become an alien in your own land. You turn a corner, the landscape changes, everyone's gone.

MARTIN: How did you die? Did they kill you?

BODY: Depends how you see it – you took rat poison, you might ask why…

MARTIN: You – I was a Catholic – what about the after-life… Suicide…

BODY: You're the Catholic, Major – not me. It's all part of our new identity.

Don't cry. Look, I'm tired now, I think I'm going off for a little swim, I'll join you later. Don't cry.

We hear the sound of MONTAGU and co return.

SCENE 6F

MONTAGU: Thank you for sharing your meagre ration of tea with us, Mr Shrieve – we should get him out into his temporary coffin now – the Squadron Leader and I have a long drive ahead of us tonight – all the way to Holy Loch.

SHRIEVE: And I hope you enjoy the show sir.

MONTAGUE: Shrieve, you must never, never breathe a word of this to anyone. Seal your lips.

SHRIEVE: You think this is the strangest thing I seen sir? Why would I wanna talk about this – happens all the time.

They exit with the body on stretcher, SHRIEVE and CHOLMONDLEY still swapping Sid Field gags:

MARTIN: I remember being undressed when I was drunk and put to bed by a lady… I remember her tenderness, her kindness… I must have been repellent to handle, smelly, dirty, probably pissed myself…

It's all coming back…

Outside we hear the song:

> 'I met a man down Aldgate.
> He'd gone funny in his head.
> He said the Nazis round up beggars…

And inject them till they're dead.
CHORUS: It wouldn't happen here, no it couldn't
happen here.'

MARTIN: I've got nowhere. I was someone, someone
important. Now I am no-one. Nobody. Not even a nobody,
just a body.

I'm a Welsh dosser. My name is Glyndwr Michael,
illegitimate son of a Thomas…, officially a lunatic vagrant
– whose life was not worth living.

CHARLIE: Oh come, we don't know that.

MARTIN: I took rat poison in a warehouse in St Pancras,
didn't I?

CHARLIE: So it would seem Major…

MARTIN: The only other possibility is even worse.

CHARLIE: The other possibility being?

MARTIN: The possibility that Burke and bloody Hare there
killed me and then used my body.

CHARLIE: Now you're getting paranoid again.

MARTIN: Am I paranoid, or are they out to get me? Eh? I
wouldn't trust those two down to the end of the street
– they're only after my body, they'd do anything to get
their mitts on me. Bastards – fucking Mincemeat –

So did it work ? Go on – tell me – what happens after this?

CHARLIE: You know I can't –

MARTIN: How much time have I got left?

CHARLIE: You have four heavenly hours.

MARTIN: I don't want to have to waste that time, ploughing
through military history – I want to know who I am, for
fuck's sake – Tell me – no-one's listening.

CHARLIE: (*He takes a breath and risks breaking the rules. Rapidly.*) After your death – your body saves thousands of lives – the Germans swallow the bait, Mincemeat Swallowed, Rod Line and Sinker, runs the message from 'Our Man in Gibraltar' – and Hitler sends a whole Panzer division from France to Greece, where it is completely unused – and points his guns on Sicily towards Sardinia – and the allied landing goes well, because of you – because of your war.

MARTIN: My war? I doubt it somehow – I'm an illegitimate, Welsh dosser.

CHARLIE: Well many people believe it is going to get better for people like you after the war – for everyone in fact.

MARTIN: I bet you that in fifty years' time, in a hundred years' time, a fucking thousand years' time, I bet you there'll still be 'people like me' out there suffering, and bastards like that won't give a toss whether I live or die. ...

Go on – what happens to Captain Ponce and Commander Shitbag in the future? I bet they don't commit suicide.

CHARLIE: Quickly then – Actually, Hitler commits suicide later – you could say partly because of you –

Beat. 'MAJOR MARTIN' is shattered.

CHARLIE: (*Tenderly.*) It was a war. (*Beat.*) You were dead. (*Beat.*) Your body saved thousands of lives.

MARTIN: My body...

Space.

CHARLIE: We could try to find some friends.....there's nothing to say you didn't have friends.

MARTIN: Who would befriend me? Smelly, dirty, stinking tramp?

CHARLIE: You are still a person – you still had a life, even if it wasn't as glamorous as you thought...come on, let's try to find out who you really were…not your name or rank…but who you really were…

MARTIN: I am the man who never was. And that is what I always was – the man who never was.

CHARLIE: Come on…

MARTIN: Well I got nothing to lose I suppose.

CHARLIE: That's the spirit.

MARTIN: … I'm dead already.

CHARLIE: I wasn't going to mention that… Come on – what about a little drink, on the way. (*They start exiting.*)

MARTIN: I like a drink.

CHARLIE: I thought you did…

MARTIN: I drink to forget.

CHARLIE: Me too…

MARTIN: I like to get away, out of this, just for a moment, just for a time.

CHARLIE: A sort of 'temporary autonomous zone'.

MARTIN: I don't know what that means…

CHARLIE: Neither do I… (*They are gone.*)

INTERVAL

Act Two

SCENE 7A

Audience enter a bombsite, including two monitors on the floor telling contemporary stories of war and homelessness. Sound. This is an installation which audience wander round for five minutes or so, like dazed survivors. Movement piece. Then workers appear to do bombsite clearance. CHARLIE and MAJOR MARTIN arrive.

MAJOR MARTIN is entirely Welsh now.

CHARLIE: So – you wanted to go down a notch or two – here we are – not exactly the Lower Depths, but heading that way. Let's try and find someone who knew you.

MARTIN: What is this place ?

CHARLIE: On the map, it is 'Kennedy Court' – a 'hostel for fallen women and men of the road' –

MARTIN: I think Jerry beat us to it.

CHARLIE: Dear oh dear – wait there – I will go and ask someone – stay there.

SCENE 7B

He goes off, leaving MARTIN.

WORKER 1: (*Hailing MAJOR MARTIN.*) Oi Captain, you looking for work?

WORKER 2: He doesn't want to work here. Pay is shit.

WORKER 1: Pay is shit. But he might find things.

WORKER 2: You a good finder Captain?

MARTIN: What do you mean?

WORKER 1: You good at digging things up?

MARTIN: Such as?

WORKER 2: Wallets.

WORKER 1: Necklaces.

WORKER 2: Ear-rings

MARTIN: You mean stealing? Things that belong to the dead?

WORKER 1: Oh, they don't care Captain.

WORKER 2: They don't care. Look in there. They're well past it.

FOREMAN: Oi – you two – leave it out.

WORKER 2: What boss?

FOREMAN: You know what I mean – leave it out! I'm won't put up with talk like that.

WORKER 1: Boss, we was just informing the captain…

FOREMAN: It's disrespectful

WORKER 1: Some people can't take a joke.

WORKER 2: Anyway, captain, you wouldn't find much dosh here. You know who lived in this place don't you?

MARTIN: No.

WORKER 1: Fallen women. Down and outs. Scrubbers and tramps

FOREMAN: O'Leary – I am not going to tell you again.

WORKER 1: Just passing the time of day –

WORKER 2: Cor – workers' bloody playtime, this is.

FOREMAN: Get back to work. Are you a relation, sir?

During the conversation that follows, the WORKERS are digging, carrying things around or whatever, joining in the conversation as they move around.

MARTIN: No, I'm not. I just came…to see what was going on down here…

FOREMAN: Bad, isn't it? People do come looking for their loved ones. Just makes it more difficult for us – sorting through the bits. The only way you can tell the women from the men is their hair.

WORKER 1: That's not how we do it.

FOREMAN: I'm going to tell you one more time, O'Leary.

Sorry about my lads, Sir – all this time clearing the dead and that – it sends you potty.

MARTIN: The dead people – there must be other things, clues you can identify them with?

FOREMAN: Oh yeah. All sorts of stuff. That's what people look for. Ornaments. Photos. Letters. Drives some of them mad.

WORKER 1: Like your friend the rat-man.

MARTIN: Who?

Much laughter.

FOREMAN: Oh, this poor bugger – its not funny really. He came to look for someone and he found them in bits. So he sits on the stones for a day and a night. Silly bastard…

MARTIN: Why?

FOREMAN: You know what he was doing?

MARTIN: Tell me.

Pause.

WORKER 2: Rats!

WORKER 1: Watching rats. We're not taking the piss now captain.

FOREMAN: With the bombing you get rats. They come out of the cellars.

WORKER 1: The fire gets them out.

FOREMAN: And this bloke is watching them. They're swarming all around him and he's sitting there like a statue.

Just as MARTIN is now.

WORKER 2: And we did find, you know, things belonging to his girlfriend or whoever she was, but he doesn't want them. Not interested.

WORKER 1: And he starts moving around the place, picking here, picking there. We don't catch on at first. You know what he was doing?

WORKER 2: Collecting up the poison.

WORKER 1: Bits of poison bait we put down for the rats.

WORKER 2: And he's picking up the bait and putting it in his pockets.

FOREMAN: We ask him what the hell he's doing and he says 'Too many, too many.' 'Too many what?' I say. And he says 'No more, no more' and he's still picking the poison. 'No more, no more. Too many dead.'

Much laughter.

MARTIN: Too many.

FOREMAN: And after a bit he wanders away.

Pause. MARTIN comes out of his reverie.

MARTIN: did you ever see this bloke again?

FOREMAN: Never – just vanished.

WORKER 1: I see him walking down Vallance Road once, like a man with a mission.

WORKER 2: You never said that.

MARTIN: What happened to him?

WORKER 1: No idea.

MARTIN: Dead?

WORKER 1: Probably living down the shelter – that's where most of them are now.

MARTIN: Which shelter?

FOREMAN: Tilbury, down Whitechapel way– it's massive, safest place for miles round here…

WORKER 2: Till a bomb hits it – is he a friend of yours?

MARTIN: Who?

WORKER 2: Charlie Chaplin over there. (*Indicating CHARLIE, who is hovering.*)

MARTIN: Oh – yes, thanks.

WORKER 2: He looks lost.

FOREMAN: Come on lads, let's finish up now, the night's coming on.

You want to get back up West now, sir – It's not good after dark round here. Cheerio.

MARTIN: Cheerio.

SCENE 7C

CHARLIE: What have you found?

MARTIN: Another trail gone cold – maybe Glyndwr was here, it sounds like him – I mean like me…

CHARLIE: Glyndwr was here – I've seen that chalked on a wall – now where was it? I know – Tilbury Shelter.

MARTIN: That's what they said too –

CHARLIE: Lets go there now and look then.

MARTIN: Surely there won't be anyone down there now
– we'll have to wait till an air raid siren goes.

CHARLIE: Oh no – some people have moved in there, lock
stock and barrel. Some of these shelters have become
permanent havens for the homeless.

MARTIN: Who runs them?

CHARLIE: They sort of run themselves – I'll show you – they
have become what you might call 'Temporary Autonmous
Zones'.

MARTIN: What?

CHARLIE: Never mind – let's go and look.

SCENE 8A

*The audience follow CHARLIE and MARTIN downstairs to the space
the play started in, which is now transformed into a shelter, mattresses
crammed against each other, many people living their own lives.
One inhabitant, edgy, dangerous – FIRESTARTER – is beating time
to some tune. All are doing various things in the shelter. Talking,
cooking, snogging, reading, writing, drawing, etc. The audience sit
on mattresses amongst them. Crammed.*

MARTIN moves to sit at FIRESTARTER's bench.

FIRESTARTER: That's mine!

He puts his feet up on the seat. MARTIN looks at him.

MARTIN: You got room enough, haven't you?

FIRESTARTER: Find your own place!

MOLLY: Keep my place warm for a bit if you like, love – I'm
on my way to visit someone. See you later Maureen. (*To
MARTIN.*) See you later love. Cheers Dicky. (*She exits.*)

MAUREEN: You not been down here before, love?

MARTIN: I don't know. Perhaps I have.

DAI: If you had, you'd remember. Fantastic company here. Fantastic…especially the ladies. We got Molly, we got Maureen – we even got Adelina Patti.

MAUREEN: Who?

DAI: Her over there, Adelina.

MAUREEN: Lorraine you mean.

LORENA: Lorena.

MAUREEN: That's what I said, Lorraine

DAI: Lovely Lorena. Refugee aren't you?

GERRY: Thought they'd locked her lot up.

MAUREEN: Stop it. Her fella's been carted off and locked up in an internment camp.

ALF: Illegal alien. One of Musso's boys.

LORENA: Shut up. He was contra-fascist. Giustizia e libertá.

FIRESTARTER: Wop.

LORENA: Shut up.

DAI: See, fantastic company. Except for him of course – Matches.

FIRESTARTER growls at DAI.

GERRY: We had Churchill in here the other night. 'London can take it!' he goes, 'London can take it! Come to build up our morale, he had.

MAUREEN: Bless him.

GERRY: And some woman at the back shouts out –

MAUREEN: – silly cow –

GERRY: You weren't even there, Maureen.

MAUREEN: But I heard about it.

GERRY: This woman shouts, 'We're the ones who're taking it, and you're out of the way of it, aren't you?'

MAUREEN: Silly cow. He's a good man, Mr Churchill...

GERRY: That's a matter of opinion.

MAUREEN: (*To MARTIN.*) You all right, love?

MARTIN: I've been walking. I am tired.

GERRY: Tired of London, tired of life – Shakespeare, *Hamlet.*

MAUREEN: You're an officer, aren't you? Not many officers come in here.

FIRESTARTER: Hey, hey, hey. I know you. You're the spy aren't you? Government spy. Finding out about us. Then you're gonna lock us up, seal us all up, get rid of us all. Aren't you? Hey, watch out everyone, there's a spy here. Look.

MAUREEN: Leave him alone, he's tired.

DAI: What's there to spy on, you silly bugger? All that's finished now.

MAUREEN: All what?

DAI: Spain.

FIRESTARTER: I'm not talking about Spain.

GERRY: Oh not again.

MAUREEN: Here we go. (*She's heard it all before.*)

DAI: Spain, the war I went to fight in. Where I got this ...

Shows gammy leg or arm. She's seen that before as well.

FIRESTARTER: Watch out everyone – there's a spy down here –

ALF: You're not one of those mass observation people, are you, come to watch how the other half lives, write it all down?

MAUREEN: Take no notice of them – I'm in charge down here, and I don't care if you're a spy or a yank or a toff – it doesn't matter, you need shelter, you take shelter.

LORENA takes a blanket to MARTIN.

Stretch out, make yourself at home.

DAI: Spain. The soldier's life.

MARTIN: You were a soldier?

MAUREEN: He was never a proper soldier – he was just a tramp till he moved in here.

DAI: You don't know.

MAUREEN: – Same for me and Matches down there.

FIRESTARTER: Somebody call me?

MAUREEN: I lived in Kennedy Court hostel, till they bombed it – we' re all the same down here, wherever you come from, no good putting on airs and graces.

DAI: Spanish Civil War I fought in. Good cause, that was.

MAUREEN: You should have stayed home with your missus, shouldn't you? Then maybe you wouldn't be half crippled.

MARTIN: What did you do in Spain?

FIRESTARTER: He was never in Spain. He's a bloody Welsh liar.

DAI: I fought there, mate. Madrid. Teruel.

He holds out his arm.

FIRESTARTER: Teruel my arse. A bloody dog bit him when he was begging door to door. Teruel. (*Dog-like growls and snapping.*)

DAI: You're out of your head, you are. Pack it in.

MAUREEN: What do you want down here, love?

MARTIN: I am making enquiries about a man called Glyndwr Michael – I believe he might have kipped around here.

FIRESTARTER: I told you he was a spy.

MARTIN: He was – my – cousin –

No-one takes the bait.

It's worth money….

DAI: (*Rapidly, warmly.*) I thought you looked like him.

MARTIN: You knew him?

MAUREEN: You never knew him.

DAI: I did so. You remember him – mad as a kite – mad Taff.

MAUREEN: Mad Taff?

DAI: You two could be brothers –

MARTIN: I'm his cousin.

MAUREEN: If it's the same mad Taff I'm thinking of, I didn't know he had family… – (*To MAJOR MARTIN.*) ain't you done well…

MARTIN: Tell me about him.

FIRESTARTER: You his cousin? That lanky scumbag owed me money.

MARTIN: Look, have whatever I have in my pockets –

Here. (*Pulls out cigarettes.*)

FIRESTARTER: What do you want?

MARTIN: Just tell me all you know about Glyndwr Michael.

MARTIN puts cigarettes on the table. FIRESTARTER divides them into three. Takes his share.

FIRESTARTER: (*Lighting up.*) You know what we was told in the Army, Captain? Salute anything that moves. (*Salutes.*) Never volunteer. And don't tell an officer nothing.

MARTIN: I'm not really an officer –

FIRESTARTER: Nothing. Nix.

MARTIN: I am the same as you people, I am one of you.

FIRESTARTER: Nought:

MARTIN: Tell me.

FIRESTARTER: Nothing. Not one word me.

MARTIN: Tell me. (*Silence.*)

MARTIN pulls out his gun. A gesture of weakness not strength.

MAUREEN: No!

FIRESTARTER: Whoa, Captain. What are you going to do with that? Whoa! Whoa!

MARTIN backs off.

Good boy.

DAI: Put the gun away. Don't be daft. – I'll tell you …

FIRESTARTER: Let's light him a candle.

DAI: Where you from?

MARTIN: I was born in Aberbargoed. I am a son of Wales.

DAI: Aberbargoed – famous place, that is. Famous. They got the biggest coal tip in the world there, don't they? Easy now, I'll tell you.

FIRESTARTER lights a candle.

FIRESTARTER: A candle for Glyndwr.

Throughout what follows, FIRESTARTER tends the candle.

SCENE 8B

DAI: I know Mad Taff off and on for years.

ALF: (*Scornful laugh.*)

DAI: No – I really did. We left Wales on the same day, September 1936. He left because his back was bad – you remember how tall he was – and he couldn't work in the colliery any more, and me – I was off to Barcelona.

LORENA: No pasaran.

FIRESTARTER laughs. DAI starts telling it to MARTIN, and then changes to telling it about him for the rest, with MARTIN playing along, as MAD TAFF.

Barcelona with the wife and her mother shouting curses at me. I never been back. Never will now... We met on the road. 'Where are you going' he says, and I says 'Spain, the war' and he says 'Are we fighting the Spaniards now?'

FIRESTARTER: Ignorant bastard.

DAI: Never knew anything, Glyndwr. So I told him about the fascists, and how one thing led to another, and how they'd be here next. And I could see that impressed him. And I gave him a bit about the workers' international. 'Workers of the world unite,' I said – this was tramping through some bloody English village, 'you have nothing to lose but your chains' (*The internationale sung again.*) And he was on fire. Like a man possessed, hopping by the side of the road.

MARTIN: (*As TAFF.*) 'Show me where these fascists are, take me to them. I'll give them a good hiding now this minute. Let me at them – bastards.'

DAI: That's right. I thought he was mad, then, like, though it wasn't anything like what came later.

Sound, bombs in background.

Anyway, eventually I calms him down and we get a lift in the back of a lorry. Takes us to Windsor. With the castle and the statue of the old queen. Two scruffy taffs sleeping in the park there with bloody deers for company. Very peaceful. Didn't do his back any good mind. And in the morning what does the silly bugger do – he sees the soldiers and the barracks, and in he goes up to the counter, and he says to the sergeant, with his back all bent up.

MARTIN: (*As TAFF.*) 'I want to fight.'

GERRY: You knew him?

DAI: And the sergeant says:

GERRY: (*Now playing the Sergeant.*) 'Come on then.'

MARTIN: (*As TAFF.*) 'No I want to fight in Spain.'

DAI: 'We don't do that,' says the sergeant.

GERRY: 'We got no quarrel with the Spanish. Maybe in a year or two.'

MARTIN: (*As TAFF.*) 'I want to go now!'

GERRY: 'Come back in a couple of years and we'll have a proper war for you. Bugger off now.'

MARTIN: (*As TAFF.*) 'I will – I'll bugger right off.' (*He sets off as if to exit.*)

GERRY: Captain – where you going? Don't go – just playing around.

DAI: And that's what he did, he walked out. And forgot all about Spain. Said he was going to get a job in London. So I went on my own. Train to Barcelona. Fighting in the trenches. Got this, got captured. Prison. No good really. And then I come back, and now I'm here. I was a soldier Maureen, I was a bloody soldier. No pasaran, Adelina, no pasaran. (*Clenched fist.*)

MARTIN: And when you came back from Spain, did you meet Glyn –... my cousin – again?

DAI: I think I saw him once in bloody Charing Cross Road singing his head off for money. Couldn't sing a note. Daft bugger. Just as daft as that one there –

MARTIN: What drove him so mad? how did he get like that?

DAI: How would I know – got no time for headcases now, me, too busy looking after myself.

FIRESTARTER looks up and makes menacing noises.

SCENE 8C

MAUREEN: I know a mad Taff, not sure if it's the same one – didn't look like you – different kettle altogether.

MARTIN: Tell me about him.

MAUREEN: I knew his lady friend, Rosa.

MARTIN: He had a lady friend?

MAUREEN: Lived on the same landing as me, in Kennedy Court. She used to stroke his head to calm him down, sing to him, tell him stories about the sea and that.

MARTIN: The sea?

MAUREEN: When he went a bit doolally. He heard noises in his head you see, poor bleeder, inside his ears. Ringing, hissing, buzzing, siren sounds.

MARTIN: From the bombing?

MAUREEN: God knows. That's why he walked, Rosa said. To wear himself out. Stop the noises.

DAI: Headcase.

Sound of Maggie Fach, Welsh song, distant.

MAUREEN: Sometimes he'd lie in her lap for hours. All night sometimes, she said. (*Beat.*)

He was away the night it happened.

MARTIN: What?

MAUREEN: Siren went, as usual, I went down the shelter sharpish – that was before I moved in here, see – and when I got back to the hostel, the whole front was gone and you could see the fires burning away inside. Lovely blue sky above. She was dead of course, my friend Rosa.

It broke him up. I see him sitting there in the ruins. I could see he was gone. Siren, he says, the noise is like a siren in my head. He doesn't talk to me apart from that.

She pauses.

FIRESTARTER makes a noise like an air-raid siren.

MOLLY returns and joins MAUREEN.

MAUREEN: (*Tired.*) Oh just shut up.

ALF: Ever see him again?

MAUREEN: I met him down the shelter after that. And held his hand and stroked his hair. Didn't do much good though did it, did it?

Pause.

MARTIN: How? What happened?

MAUREEN: Oh it's too much. I want to go home. I want to go home.

MARTIN: What happened?

MAUREEN: Nothing happened. That's it.

VOICE FROM SURFACE: (*Shouts down.*) Everything alright down there?

ANOTHER VOICE: Yes.

FIRESTARTER: It's all lies and propaganda – don't believe a word of it.

MARTIN: What?

FIRESTARTER: Neither of them knew him. I knew him. I shared a fucking room with him. Forget this 'Mad Taff' business – I know the bloke you mean – Owain Glyndwr he called himself, something like that. He's dead now.

MARTIN: How did he die? Did he kill himself?

FIRESTARTER: Slow down. Take it easy. I'll tell you.

MARTIN: Everything?

FIRESTARTER: All I know. Now Welsh is a bloody liar, she's a bloody liar and I'm a bloody liar. But this is true. God's honest truth. So help me.

MARTIN: When did you …?

FIRESTARTER: I shared a room with him, me and fifteen others. Owain Glyndwr was a thief. Took my money and gave me nothing but grief. I had to knock him about a few times. Then he toddles off to his bed and lies there crying. Two or three times at least, this happened, he never would learn his lesson.

LORENA: Poverino. Che crudele che sei.

FIRESTARTER: One night it's different. He's taken to staying out in the bombsites when the sirens go, going nice and crazy. And he comes back with his pockets full of ratbait – poison. Saving the rats, do you see? And when he gets back, it's like he can't stop himself, he dips into my pocket – jacket pocket – helps himself to two and six. Two and six! So I have to go for him, teach him a lesson again. Which I do. And he goes off to bed again. He's crying. But this time, this time, the crying starts to sound different. It's not – (*He demonstrates sobs.*) – it's – (*He demonstrates howls, repeatedly, in anguish.*) You know what the stupid bastard had done? Taken the rat poison. He was dying like one of his bloody rats.

MARTIN: Oh God!

Starts to make sounds that are an echo of the howling.

FIRESTARTER: Stupid bastard. It goes on for half the bloody day.

MOLLY: 'Call the ambulance,'

FIRESTARTER: That's what one of my mates says. 'And have the police here too? Not bloody likely,' I say.

MOLLY: 'Call the ambulance!'

FIRESTARTER: 'Fuck off!'

ALF: 'Call an ambulance!'

FIRESTARTER: 'Fuck off!' And bloody Taffy's howling away. We couldn't stand it. Went down the shelter. When we get back, they're carrying him out, with a bloody hankie over his face. Thank God. Poor bastard.

Pause.

MARTIN: Where'd they put him?

Where is he buried?

FIRESTARTER: Buried? You think he's buried, Captain? Where have you come from? Don't you know what they do with dead beggars? 'Donated to medical science' – (*Pause.*) They cut us up… Or something like that.

SCENE 8D

CHARLIE: So – your time is almost up. Now you know.

MARTIN fights him and imaginary others off. He is possessed.

MARTIN/GLYNDWR: Get your hands off me…fucking get away from me…you fucking English bastards… I know you, I know your type…you're going to cut me up, aren't you, you're going to cut me into little pieces.

CHARLIE: It's me, your friend, your guide.

MARTIN/GLYNDWR: You bastards are all the fucking same… well you got me wrong though, didn"t you…none of you know who I really am… I'll tell you who I really am… I am the reincarnation of Owain fucking Glyndwr, Owain fucking Glyndwr, true Prince of Wales, Son of Prophecy.

'At my nativity
The front of heaven was full of fiery shapes,
Of burning cressets, and at my birth
The frame and huge foundation of the earth
Shak'd like a coward'

CHARLIE: Wonderful, wonderful – you've really found yourself.

MARTIN/GLYNDWR: 'Of many men
I do not bear these crossings; give me leave
To tell you once again that at my birth
The front of heaven was full of fiery shapes
The goats ran from the mountains, and the herds
Were strangely clamorous to the frighted fields.
These signs have mark'd me extraordinary,
And all the courses of my life do show
I am not in the roll of common men…'

CHARLIE: *Henry Four Part One.* Owain Glendower. Well done. Let us go. They're ready for you.

They set off in step and then stop.

(*To audience.*) That is what is known as a false ending. Next false ending.

MARTIN: Tie up the loose ends.

CHARLIE: What?

MARTIN: Am I famous?

CHARLIE: After the war, Commander Montagu will write a book describing this operation, *The Man Who Never Was,* which was then made into a film, from which he made a lot of money.

MARTIN: But am I famous?

CHARLIE: He never revealed your identity.

MARTIN: So no-one knows.

CHARLIE: In the book he claimed you were a naval officer
– he says 'I swore to his relatives that I would never reveal
his identity, and since there is no living person from whom
I can secure a release, I will therefore take the secret
honourably to the grave with me…' Your identity only
came to light in 1997, when papers were released.

MARTIN: 44 years. But I made it didn't I? The hall of fame.
The spotlight of history.

CHARLIE: Yes, the spotlight picked you out. They put up a
plaque to you in Aberbargoed.

MARTIN: A plaque!

CHARLIE: But then, I have to say –

MARTIN: What?

CHARLIE: There were other stories. An exploded warship in
Scotland, an unmarked corpse. A last minute substitution
perhaps… We have not been able to find out.

MARTIN: Know thyself. My 24 hours are almost up.

CHARLIE: Well some say they might have dumped poor old
Glyndwr's body on the way up to Holy Loch, and loaded
up a nice fresh one, belonging to a Scottish sailor from an
aircraft carrier which exploded.

MARTIN: Don't tell me that.

CHARLIE: So you might not even be Glyndwr.

MARTIN: I am who I am, you can't take that away from me.
They got it wrong. I am Glyndwr, son of Wales, I know
myself and I like myself.

CHARLIE: Fair enough.

MARTIN: What about the spook?

CHARLIE: He refuses to have any part of the book deal, turns down a share of the profits, stays in the secret service the rest of his life.

MARTIN: So Montagu is willing to share the money with Cholmondley – does my family get any of it? Does any family?

CHARLIE: Well, according to Montagu –

MARTIN: There are no living relatives – sure thing.

CHARLIE: (*To audience.*) And now the last end. (*To MARTIN.*) After you.

MARTIN: Do Chaplin.

CHARLIE: OK – why not? The last speech from *The Great Dictator.* Just the words.

'I'm sorry but I don't want to be an emperor. That's not my business. I don't want to rule or conquer anyone. I should like to help everyone if possible: Jew, Gentile, black men, white. We all want to help one another. Human beings are like that. We want to live by each others' happiness, not by each other's misery. We don't want to hate and despise one another. In this world there is room for everyone. And the good earth is rich and can provide for everyone. The way of life can be free and beautiful, but we have lost the way.'

Projected on the street doors through which the van drove in the first scene, we see projected the film of the very last passage of The Great Dictator. *CHAPLIN speaking.*

CHAPLIN: We are coming out of the darkness into the light! We are coming into a new world; a kind new world, where men will rise above their hate, their greed, and brutality. Look up, Hanna! The soul of man has been given wings and at last he is beginning to fly. He is flying into the rainbow. Into the light of hope! Into the future! The glorious future! That belongs to you, to me, and to all of us. Look up, Hanna! Look up!

The doors open in the last phrase, and CHARLIE and MARTIN exit.

RECORDED VOICE: Mincemeat.

Blackout.

THE END